Strategic Advising
in Foreign Assistance

Pamela,
Thank you for
the opportunity
to work in this
space —
Nadia

STRATEGIC ADVISING
in Foreign Assistance

A PRACTICAL GUIDE

Nadia Gerspacher

 Kumarian Press

A Division of Lynne Rienner Publishers, Inc. • Boulder & London

Published in the United States of America in 2016 by
Kumarian Press
A division of Lynne Rienner Publishers, Inc.
1800 30th Street, Boulder, Colorado 80301
www.rienner.com

and in the United Kingdom by
Kumarian Press
A division of Lynne Rienner Publishers, Inc.
3 Henrietta Street, Covent Garden, London WC2E 8LU

Library of Congress Cataloging-in-Publication Data
Names: Gerspacher, Nadia, author.
Title: Strategic advising in foreign assistance : a practical guide / by
    Nadia Gerspacher.
Description: Boulder, Colorado : Kumarian Press, a division of Lynne Rienner
    Publishers, Inc., 2016. | Includes bibliographical references and index.
Identifiers: LCCN 2015043551| ISBN 9781626375215 (hardcover : alk. paper) |
    ISBN 9781626375222 (pbk. : alk. paper)
Subjects: LCSH: Nation building. | Institution building. | Economic
    assistance.
Classification: LCC JZ6300 .G47 2016 | DDC 327.1/11—dc23
LC record available at http://lccn.loc.gov/2015043551

British Cataloguing in Publication Data
A Cataloguing in Publication record for this book
is available from the British Library.

Printed and bound in the United States of America

The paper used in this publication meets the requirements
of the American National Standard for Permanence of
Paper for Printed Library Materials Z39.48-1992.

5 4 3 2 1

In memory of
Norman L. Melnikoff

Contents

Preface

ADVISING HAS BECOME A KEY COMPONENT OF INTERNATIONAL interventions in postconflict, postrevolution, transitioning states. It can also be effective in preventing conflict, addressing state fragility, and helping governments to recover from crises and disasters. Advising as a strategy to enhance government capacity has been used for at least half a century: the United States employed advisers in its war in Vietnam; NATO's post–Cold War Partnership for Peace program in former Soviet states and elsewhere relied heavily on advisers; and more recently, advisers have featured in the international interventions in Iraq and Afghanistan. Yet, the international community still operates mostly in an ad hoc manner when it comes to deploying advisers—even though these men and women can significantly strengthen government capacity and societal stability at a fraction of the cost of other types of intervention. Many sets of guidelines are available for different approaches to development, diplomacy, and defense, but no guidelines are dedicated to the art of advising. In this book, I attempt to fill that void.

The material in the book has been developed over five years of working directly with advisers from the United States, Canada, and European countries. I have conducted needs assessments for the training of advisers, developed curriculum for courses, and taught military and civilian advisers who have been recruited to work in the development community, the security sector, and other sectors. I have also debriefed many advisers returning from their tours and provided support to many others during their deployments, affording me valuable insight into the challenges that they face and the tools that they need to assist their counterparts. I have engaged think tanks, government agencies, and international organizations on good practices, lessons learned, and guidelines and have organized conferences, all with the goal of further understanding the advising mission.

In addition to working with advisers and their deploying agencies, I have sought out "counterparts"—officials from ministries in various countries who have worked with advisers. These counterparts have shared how and why they grant access to and use some advisers as resources to strengthen their institutions. For the most part, they recount negative experiences, including advisers who tried to take over the running of a ministry, advisers who showed no respect for the systems and practices already in place, and advisers who insisted that their own systems were superior and should be emulated. The counterparts also explained how the donor community at large conducts itself in highly insensitive ways and seems unable to understand the local context, its opportunities, and its limitations.

All this listening has informed the material presented in this book. Indeed, the book calls for a significant shift in the attitudes that advisers bring to their missions, and it offers advisers guidance on how to improve both their reputations and their ability to truly assist.

The book could have been structured in a variety of ways. I chose an approach that emphasizes three categories of assets: awareness, knowledge, and tools. These categories are interdependent and woven throughout the book. They are meant to empower advisers and those who draft their mandates to approach their capacity-building function responsibly, sensitively, capably, and creatively.

* * *

This book is the result of much of my work at the United States Institute of Peace. The USIP leadership and my education and training colleagues in the USIP Academy for International Conflict Management and Peacebuilding provided considerable support for the programs from which the book emerged, as well as both the writing and publication processes.

I would like to thank Pamela Aall, the former provost of the USIP Academy for International Conflict Management and Peace-building, for having the vision to see the need to develop a body of knowledge about how advisers and mentors can engage local actors more effectively and without doing harm.

I would also like to thank Jeff Helsing for his suggestions during the process of curriculum development of the many advising courses I have designed, and for his support of USIP's work with advisers and mentors and of this book.

Special thanks go to my editor, Nigel Quinney, whose feedback was constructive, thought provoking, and extremely useful throughout the writing process.

I am grateful to Courtney McCreesh, my invaluable research assistant, for her tireless and enthusiastic contributions in the form of research and editing assistance throughout the entire process of writing this book.

I would like to thank all those who have endorsed the material that I have developed over the past five years and those who have used these guidelines in their advising activities. They include my students at the USIP Academy; the Ministry of Defense Advisor's (MoDA) program; the US Department of State's Bureau of International Narcotics and Law Enforcement (INL); the German Zentrum Internationale Friedenseinsatze (ZIF); the Scuola Sant'Anna in Pisa, Italy; and the International Association of Peacekeeping Training Centers (IAPTC). A special thanks goes to those who shared their experiences and anecdotes and helped to make this material more concrete: Josh Burgess, David Clifton, Paolo Costa, Rasheed Diallo, George Dryden, Mark Downes, Wendy Fontella, John Gilette, Jay Hawk, Chuck Heiden, Gordon Hughes, Mark Jones, Erik Leklem, Natacha Meden, Teohna Williams, and Scott Wilson. I am also indebted to the former ministers and other officials who shared their stories, good and bad, of interactions with foreign advisers.

Special thanks also go to many others: A. Heather Coyne, who took my first class on this subject in 2009 and who not only recognized the relevance of the material to the missions of the many advisers deployed in Iraq and Afghanistan, but also helped me develop invaluable contacts with former advisers willing to share valuable lessons and to draw up a wish list of what they would have liked to have known before they deployed. The Center for Complex Operations, especially Jacqueline Carpenter, for the focus group opportunities that led to the development of an ideal curriculum for advisers. Those who already recognized the need for better training of advisers and who have incorporated this material in their training programs, including David Cate, Annalisa Creta, Andrea De Gutty, George Dryden, Claudia Munoz, Jim Schear, Eleanor Pavey, Kelly Uribe, and Petra Van Oijen, and Mark Downes. My colleagues at USIP who have contributed their expertise to various advising programs and from whom current and future advisers have acquired key skills. The many people who have participated in the US Army Building Partner Capacity (BPC) TRADOC/ARCIC Capabilities-Based Assessment working group; the group's insights have been very useful in understanding the challenges inherent in working with foreign counterparts. Michael Riha, who provided me a firsthand look at the development of the BPC US Army doctrine, and Col. Timothy Russell and the US Army for the recognition of the importance of this material in the 2013 FM 3-22 Guide to Security Cooperation.

Finally, I would like to thank my parents, Michel and Doris Gerspacher, for giving me the chance to live and work with individuals from different cultures and backgrounds and to learn to work adaptably. I hope that what I learned, as reflected in this book, will be useful for those whose duties require them to live and work alongside people from other countries and cultures.

1

Introduction

THIS BOOK OFFERS A PRACTICAL INTRODUCTION TO THE ART OF "strategic advising." Strategic advising is a tool used by the international community to build the capacity of governments to govern societies emerging from conflict or transitioning from authoritarian to democratic regimes. A strategic adviser is sent by the international community to work alongside a high-ranking official in a transitional or postconflict state and offer guidance that can contribute to the development of effective policies and procedures. Like the related but distinctively different tasks of training and mentoring, strategic advising is fundamentally an exercise in transferring knowledge. Transferring knowledge is just one of the approaches to strengthening capacity in fragile or postconflict environments, but it is a key component.

Capacity-building endeavors are not new, but the way in which they are conducted is. The old model of building capacity entailed transferring capital and individuals from stable, wealthy countries to unstable, usually poor countries to implement foreign assistance projects. That model is now largely discredited and has been replaced by a paradigm that emphasizes the transfer of knowledge, skills, and information. However, there is no consensus on which knowledge, skills, and information should be shared. In many instances, for example, the only skills that are shared are those required to use the

1

new equipment that has been transferred as part of a foreign-assistance package. This approach is gradually coming to be recognized as the final—not the first—step in an effective capacity-building strategy.[1]

Another problem posed by the current approach to knowledge transfer is that it recruits practitioners who are undoubtedly expert in their subject areas, but who are not trained to impart that expertise in a way that local officials will find helpful. The judges, police officers, logistics experts, human resources professionals, and other practitioners who are recruited and deployed know how to manage programs in their own systems, but that expertise is not necessarily relevant to the contexts and cultures in which they find themselves. Moreover, they are doers, not teachers; they are accustomed to getting things done in the way they want them done, not to giving others advice and options that may well be ignored or discarded.

If they are to be effective, strategic advisers need to learn *how* to transfer knowledge and how to mitigate the dynamics that threaten the completion of their mission. For example, a US police officer may have much to offer when it comes to sharing practices and procedures for investigating crimes, strengthening a case so that it is admissible in court, and arresting an alleged perpetrator while respecting civil and human rights. And these skills can be significant assets to a transitional society—but only if they are used to help prepare the individuals in the host society who will actually carry out reforms in that country. The police officer–turned–capacity builder will not practice his craft in the capacity-strengthening mission. Instead, he must act as an information and knowledge broker. A knowledge broker's job is to identify and diagnose needs or gaps in the local system, and to draw from his experience ideas and approaches that fit the local context and can contribute to the functioning of the local system.

The transfer of knowledge, skills, and information is a complex process with many moving parts. It requires a keen understanding of the various factors that can indicate success or failure. This book provides that understanding. In doing so, it fills a gap in the literature. Advising is only slowly coming to be seen as a separate practice from training and mentoring, and in the past advisers had few resources to which they could turn for advice on how to perform their specific role. To create such a resource, I conducted a series of comprehensive needs assessments and focus groups, debriefed numerous returning advisers, and drew on the knowledge and expertise acquired over five years spent helping to prepare advisers as capacity builders for their missions. I also mined various disciplines and fields such as international education, project planning, social work, and international development for relevant ideas and insights, knowledge, and tools.

This book is not a review of past or current practice; instead, it draws on the lessons of the past to develop a new, more effective approach to strategic advising. It offers a conceptual framework within which to understand the role of the strategic adviser, presents a fund of practical advice on how to perform that role, and lays out a variety of tools that can be used in the field. It explains how to make the shift from an experienced practitioner who practices his craft to a knowledge broker who participates in reform efforts by contributing ideas and supporting the process of planning and implementing reform of government institutions and policies. In short, this book describes what a high-quality adviser looks and acts like and what she hopes to accomplish.

This book is divided into ten chapters (plus a short conclusion), the order of which follows the logic of the advising mission. The book begins where any advising mission should begin: by developing a clear understanding that such a mission is fundamentally a capacity-building activity (Chapter 2), and that it requires the transformation of a practitioner into an adviser (Chapter 3). The book then accompanies the adviser when she arrives in country and begins to develop relationships with the relevant actors, including local officials, stakeholders (such as the officials' staffs), potential beneficiaries of an enhanced service, other agencies that need to be involved in reform efforts, and a variety of international organizations and their staffs.

From the start of the deployment, the adviser needs to manage her expectations, anticipate a variety of commonly encountered dilemmas, nurture institutional buy-in, and start establishing authority, credibility, and legitimacy (Chapter 4). At the same time, the adviser must assess what capacity already exists locally (Chapter 5), thereby beginning to build an in-depth understanding of the local situation, developing respect for what capacity already exists, and avoiding proposing ideas that have already been tried. Equally important is identifying the local actors who will play key roles in the process of change, either as partners in promoting change, as the targets of change, or as agents of change (Chapter 6).

Equipped with this understanding of local realities, the adviser can then press ahead with the task of knowledge sharing. To accomplish this task effectively, the adviser must not only possess expert knowledge but also know how to transfer that knowledge. The effective adviser appreciates the importance of dialogue, is familiar with the methods and principles of adult learning, and is sensitive to the trauma that many local actors will have experienced (Chapter 7). Relationship building lies at the heart of the adviser's work, especially the task of building a relationship with the adviser's "counterpart"—the official whom the adviser has been deployed to work alongside and support. The adviser must be aware of the various stages through which the adviser-counterpart relationship should progress, and must be careful to adopt a constructive, supportive, respectful approach at each of those stages. Throughout, he must recognize the essential elements of an effective working relationship: mutual respect, trust, good rapport, cultural adaptability, language sensitivity, capable interpreters, denationalized models, and professional distance (Chapter 8).

The adviser has to work within an environment crammed with a multitude of actors with differing interests, goals, approaches, and cultures. Learning how to coordinate with these actors, especially the international ones, is invaluable if the adviser wants to avoid duplicating, complicating, undermining, or being undermined by the work of those actors (Chapter 9).

All the adviser's efforts will count for nothing if they do not continue to bear fruit when the adviser's deployment ends and she heads home. In other words, the adviser needs, from the start to the completion of her mission, to build sustainability into her capacity-building activities. Promoting sustainability requires recognizing the major obstacles to the development of sustainable systems and solutions, and abiding by principles that make it possible to overcome those obstacles in each of the five phases of the advising mission (Chapter 10).

The switchover between an outgoing and an incoming adviser can be a trying time for everyone concerned, including the counterpart and his staff, who may see projects nurtured by the outgoing adviser neglected by her replacement, and whose patience may be taxed by a new arrival who wants to ask the same questions that were already answered for the benefit of the outgoing adviser. To ensure that her work is not wasted and that the confidence of local actors in the advising mission is not severely dented, the outgoing adviser should engage in continuity planning. This involves carefully documenting the information that the adviser acquired at each of the five phases, and passing this documentation on to the incoming adviser (Chapter 11).

The book directly addresses strategic advisers, yet the awareness, knowledge, and tools presented in the following chapters should be of interest to anyone working to support change in transitional societies. To build capacity in society, everyone—from foreign advisers to local elites to everyday citizens—needs certain tools and skills. While numerous international bodies and many US agencies agree that capacity building is vital, until now there has not been a book that offers an academically well-informed and practitioner-friendly explanation of how to build capacity. The ultimate goal of this book is to help everyone working to promote well-functioning government institutions capable of delivering enhanced services to citizens and of managing conflict peacefully.

Note

1. David H. Bayley and Robert M. Perito, *Police in War: Fighting Insurgency, Terrorism, and Violent Crime* (Boulder, CO: Lynne Rienner, 2010).

2

What Is Capacity Building?

ADVISING IS ONE OF THE TOOLS WITH WHICH THE INTERNA-
tional community seeks to build or rebuild the capacity of transitional societies and societies emerging from conflict. Capacity building lies at the core of most interventions conducted by the
international community today, and advising is a means to achieve
enhanced capacity. But what, exactly, is *capacity*? Why is capacity so
important to a society? What does *capacity building* mean and what
does it entail? Why does the international community make it such a
high priority? And what lessons is the international community learning from its past experiences in trying to strengthen capacity? This
chapter tackles each of these questions in turn.

What Is Capacity and Why Is It
So Important to a Society?

Capacity consists of the various functions and systems that coexist
peacefully and productively in a "capable" society. A capable society
is one in which a host of orderly, predictable activities take place on
a daily basis. Children go to school, adults to work, consumers to
stores, students go to college, the sick go to hospital, and so forth.
The society has a set of rules and a mechanism for enforcing them.
The capable society has a justice system, complete with police offi-

cers, defense counsel, judges, and all the other personnel required; a functioning transportation infrastructure maintained by skilled workers; a system of communications that includes post offices and cell phone towers. In a capable society, needs are identified and systems that address them are put into place. The public expects government services and the government strives to provide them.

The capacity of government institutions to deliver basic services to the population systematically, reliably, and equitably is not only necessary to the conduct of daily life but also crucial to prevent the outbreak of violent conflict. Violence often erupts because there are no established channels within a country's governance structure through which to voice dissent, to rally forces opposed to the government, and to promote a national discourse on issues that affect peoples' lives.[1] This lack of capacity to address conflict peacefully manifests itself in a myriad of ways: lack of capacity to educate future staff and officials of institutions and agencies, lack of capacity to mediate and resolve political and other disputes, and so forth.

A capable society requires not only a government with the capacity to provide a stable and reliable environment but also an array of civil society actors, such as media, universities, and watchdog groups, to monitor the government's performance. These actors and their dynamics form a complex web. This complexity is best understood when capacity is disaggregated into three interrelated levels: individual, institutional, and societal:

- At the individual level, capacity consists of an ability to perform specific tasks effectively and thereby contribute to the functioning of the overall system.
- At the institutional level, capacity consists of structural policies, procedures, and practices that support, manage, and administer a service to the population reliably, equitably, and systematically. Institutions only function when competent and well-trained employees staff them. An institutional system, process, or procedure should be structured to adapt, absorb, and utilize the capacities that individuals can offer.
- At the societal level, capacity consists of having a pool of individuals who can contribute to the effective functioning of government, other organizations, and society as a whole.

What Does Capacity Building Mean and What Does It Entail?

Although *capacity building* has no agreed-upon definition within the international community, this book offers one that is meant to be instructive for anyone engaging in capacity-building activities. Capacity building is a process by which people, institutions, and societies can develop, strengthen, and expand their ability to meet their goals or fulfill their mandates. Typical approaches to capacity building include the deployment of trainers, advisers, mentors, and even expert teams. Most existing organizational definitions focus on the approach taken by that organization to capacity building to define the term, which has caused confusion and complicated the process of planning missions. The United Nations Development Programme (UNDP) regards capacity building as a long-term, continual process in which all stakeholders participate.[2] The capacity-building work of the UNDP rests on a three-tiered model: (1) unlocking the potential of a society through the drafting and enactment of policies and legal structures; (2) building institutions and community organizations (particularly ones that empower women); and (3) developing human resources and strengthening oversight and managerial systems. The UNDP approach is a holistic approach to human development through capacity building.[3]

The UK's Department for International Development (DFID) defines capacity building as "involving individual and organizational learning to build social capital and trust, and to develop knowledge, skills, and attitudes in order to create an organizational culture that allows organizations or groups to set objectives, achieve results, solve problems, and give organizations the adaptability and the flexibility necessary for long-term survival."[4]

The European Union also recognizes the importance of human and social development. The EU approach to capacity building focuses on the interdependence of economic development and social progress.[5] This perspective puts human and social welfare in the context of our globalized economy. The US Agency for International Development (USAID) focuses in its capacity-building work on strengthening core public administration capacity at both the national and subnational level. The goal is to enable public-sector institutions to deliver basic public services in an effective and transparent manner.[6]

Despite their differences, these definitions focus on the ability of individuals and institutions to carry out their tasks and of societies to meet the needs of their citizens. Just as *capacity* can be disaggregated into these three levels (individual, institutional, societal), so can *capacity building*:

- At the individual level, capacity-building activities build social capital to perform tasks in the sectors of health, education, security, finance, and industry.
- At the institutional level, capacity building enhances the ability of individuals and institutions to identify solutions to problems over time.
- At the societal level, capacity-building activities foster opportunities for people to staff the institution, both now and in the future (e.g., incorporating civic education in the schooling curriculum could build capacity by fostering in young people an understanding of the government's role in providing services).

Many capacity-building activities have limited impact because they focus on only one of these levels (usually, the individual level). Training people to use computer software is an example of capacity building at the individual level. But such training will have only a limited and short-term value unless it is complemented by appropriate institutional and societal change, such as creating the technological infrastructure to repair computers and encouraging society as a whole to embrace computer technology. While it is important for the adviser to strengthen the capacity of the individuals who staff a specific institution at a given time, it is just as important to strengthen the society so that it can produce—and continue to produce—individuals who have the skills, knowledge, and sense of civic duty to staff government institutions.

At the institutional level, capacity building can be further disaggregated and decentralized into a variety of sublevels: national government institutions (such as ministries of defense and justice), local government institutions (such as police stations and school districts), and civil society organizations (such as the media, women's organizations, and professional associations). Effective capacity building usually depends on action being taken at more than one of these sublevels. For example, if capacity is built in the educational system at the local institutional level but not the national institutional level, then school districts will not be able to depend on the ministry of education for logistics, procurement, human resources, and funding. At the same time, the media and watchdog organizations must ensure that the ministry remains accountable to the public and empowers teachers to understand their roles as providers of a government service.

Recognizing that all levels and all systems within those levels are interconnected is one of the first steps toward building capacity in any country—and one to which the effective adviser pays careful attention if he is not to have a negative impact on one or more systems. A system is an organized collection of parts, or subsystems, that are highly integrated to accomplish an overall goal.[7] The system has various inputs that go through processes to produce outputs, which together accomplish the overall goal for the system. If one part of the system is altered, the nature of the overall system will likely change as well. Complex systems such as social systems are composed of numerous subsystems that are arranged in hierarchies and integrated to accomplish the overall goals of the whole system.

In a system, dynamics are in place that affect each other and form a larger pattern that is different from any of its parts. The fundamental notion of a system features continual stages of input, throughput (processing of input), and output. A system can be open or closed. A closed system does not interact with its environment and does not take in information. Closed systems are likely to vanish over time because they cannot adapt. Conversely, an open sys-

---

What Constitutes a System?

A pile of sand is not a system. If you remove a sand particle, you still have a pile of sand. However, a functioning car is a system. Remove the spark plugs and you no longer have a working car.

tem absorbs information and uses it to interact dynamically with its environment.

Once the adviser understands how to perceive a system, he should also become sensitive to the impact of the intervention on the status quo. Conflict sensitivity means being sensitive to the potential impact of advising activities (including analysis and assessment) on a specific community. Greater conflict sensitivity enhances the success of a project and minimizes potential unintended consequences. Challenges arise in capacity-strengthening projects when aid programs are inadequately designed for the specific context. Too often, there is too little investment in producing comprehensive, integrated analyses of the local content and its dynamics; as a consequence, project designs are often unrealistic, ineffective, or even counterproductive. Capacity builders should focus on systematic project design, implementation, and evaluation.

Why Is Capacity Building a High Priority for the International Community?

It is no exaggeration to say that most international interventions today are, in one way or another, capacity-strengthening missions. Why? There are three major reasons. First, the recent surge in capacity building reflects perceived inadequacies of previous approaches to reconstruction and stabilization. Many critics have accused interventions conducted during the past two decades of being ineffective, because they have sought to transplant preexisting solutions from other countries instead of devoting the time and effort to developing home-grown, sustainable solutions.[8]

The second reason lies in the advantages that a capacity-building approach brings. One of these advantages is that conflict prevention, conflict management, and conflict resolution all require significant levels of capacity. International efforts to stabilize and reconstruct transitional societies or societies emerging from conflict thus seek to develop capacity among all the stakeholder groups in a society.[9] Furthermore, as donor countries find themselves with fewer funds to commit to international assistance, they are prioritizing conflict *prevention* efforts. And prevention efforts depend heavily on developing capacity—for example, building the capacity of government institutions to discipline security forces that abuse human rights and thereby provoke rebellions.

In a time of tight budgets, capacity-building activities are also becoming the tool of choice for the development of good governance practices and development assistance. Capacity building can offer donor governments a good return on their investments in foreign assistance. The advising activities that support the development of strong government institutions and a robust civil society are less expensive than many other means of assistance, especially the provision of military assistance. The result of effective capacity building is good governance, stability, and a public that sees its government as legitimate because it can deliver services.

The third advantage of capacity building, when undertaken by advisers who are sensitive to local cultures and contexts, is that it supports the development of partnerships and networks between governments. Donor governments whose institutions are relatively effective at contributing to stability make good partners for governments trying to achieve greater stability. If they are open to suggestions, recipient governments can greatly benefit from the lessons learned by donor governments.[10]

The advantages of capacity building first began to be recognized by the international community in the immediate aftermath of the Cold War. Since then, the stock of capacity building has risen markedly, especially after it became evident in the 1990s that intrastate violent conflicts were outpacing interstate conflicts.[11] The UN, for example, has tried to harness the power of capacity building to forestall violent conflict in various ways. A paper published in 1999 by the UN, for example, argued that strong institutions can reduce corruption and thereby prevent conflict by encouraging actors to work within institutional structures and procedures.[12] The UN also has a strong track record of incorporating preventive measures into its capacity-building work in conflict-susceptible regions. The Capacity Building in Conflict Management project, for example, ran from 1999 to 2004 and had as its "overall objective" the development of "diagnostic, analytical, planning, and training instruments that will help African governments and their civil society partners to formulate proactive policies and strategies for managing disputes and diversity in their societies in preemptive, constructive, non-violent ways."[13]

Other international actors have developed an appreciation of the value of capacity building. For instance, the European Union has missions in Eastern European countries such as Moldova and Ukraine that are intended to build those countries' capacity to control their borders. The EU missions give advice on institutional procedures and systems, offer training in border control, and facilitate cooperation with other relevant actors such as Europol. NATO helps various militaries strengthen the ability of their naval forces to perform counterpiracy operations. The African Union works on capacity-building projects designed to strengthen the ability of African governments to formulate sound policy.

Learning from Past Capacity-Building Efforts

Despite the growing realization that capacity building is far superior to the "Band-Aid" approach to intervention, there is still much to be learned about how best to go about building capacity. Regrettably but inevitably, mistakes continue to be made. The US military, for example, has been heavily and directly involved in capacity building of the police in several countries emerging from conflict. As a consequence, those police forces have acquired a military outlook, seeing enemies within the public rather than criminal elements from which the public needs protection. Such a perspective makes the public wary of the police and, by extension, of the government, thereby undercutting capacity-building efforts.

A number of government agencies and multilateral organizations have sought to distill lessons for the future from the shortcomings of past missions. The United Nations and the Organization for Security and Cooperation in Europe, as well as various national agencies such as DFID and the US Department of Defense, have made important strides in capacity-building research and have begun to create a set of best practices.

Many in the international community have come to believe that the most efficient form of capacity building is one that quickly advances the capacity of local actors (individuals and institutions) to respond to their own crises and challenges. The US military has been at the forefront of the push for a "lighter footprint." A lighter footprint entails the deployment of noncombat personnel or a small team of highly competent experts who can have a big impact and be a multiplier force by imparting knowledge and helping to develop a well-functioning system that assists local officials and citizens in the development of solutions to the problems they face. For example, rather than merely exporting medical equipment for doctors or protection equipment for police, that equipment is provided only after an effective medical or policing system has been put in place. The latest US military research and practice is exemplified in the Joint Services manual *Multi-Service Tactics, Techniques, and Procedures for Advising Foreign Forces*[14] and the US Army's Field Manual 3-22, which guides operations in security cooperation.

The Ministry of Defense Advisors Program (MoDA) run by the Defense Security Cooperation Agency also reflects current thinking. As described on the MoDA website, the MoDA Program

> is designed to forge long-term relationships that strengthen a partner state's defense ministry. The program matches senior Department of Defense civilians with foreign counterparts in similar defense specialties. Ultimately, the MoDA program helps partners build core competencies that support effective and accountable defense ministries. MoDA advisors strengthen the capacity of institutions by helping counterparts to solve problems in areas that include defense policy and strategy, force planning and resource allocation, personnel and readiness management, civil-military and interagency operations, doctrine, training, and education, acquisitions and procurement, logistics, health care administration, and information, technology.[15]

A number of guidelines and agreements on "what to do" have now been developed, but there is still a need for guidance on "how to do it." For example, it is now conventional wisdom that the local solution is the only one that will be sustainable and viable from a fiscal and logistical perspective. So how does the capacity builder promote the identification of the local solution? This has proven to be a significant challenge in every capacity-building mission. Capacity builders are not often inherently proficient at identifying the local solution. But this is a skill they can acquire through training, and once mastered, can translate into real impact on foreign officials and their institutions.

A related lesson that the international community is taking to heart is the need for "local ownership": local solutions must not only be identified, they must also be implemented in a way that makes local officials feel as though they own that solution. But a clear definition of local ownership has always been elusive, due to the complex and shifting relationships among external donors, recipient national governments, and citizens on the ground.[16] It can be hard to draw the line between "appropriate" knowledge transfer (i.e., knowledge transfer that addresses a specific problem in a specific context with specific resources and constraints) and "inappropriate" donor-mandated policies and procedures, which grant too much power to the donor country. To cultivate local ownership, some experts have called for long-term capacity building that relies on training mechanisms and promotes the gradual assumption of routine functions and tasks by local actors.[17] Relatedly, many practitioners and scholars call for giving international nongovernmental organizations (NGOs) more funding independence and flexibility so that development programs can be decided by assessing local needs, not dictated by external preferences.[18] At the heart of all such proposals is the recognition that local authorities must be empowered to propose, plan, and implement solutions that are tailored to their unique environment.

Notes

1. Peter Harris and Ben Reilly, eds., *Democracy and Deep-Rooted Conflict: Options for Negotiators,* International IDEA Book Series no. 3 (Stockholm: IDEA, 1998).

2. UNDP, *Capacity Development: A UNDP Primer* (New York: UNDP, 2009), 20.

3. Ibid., 11.

4. *DFID Research Strategy 2008–2013,* Working Paper Series: Capacity Building (DFID and Research for Development, April 2008), 3, http://r4d.dfid.gov.uk/PDF/Outputs/Consultation/ResearchStrategyWorkingPaper final_capacity_P1.pdf.

5. "The European Consensus on Development: Joint Statement by the Council and the Representatives of the Governments of the Member States Meeting within the Council, the European Parliament and the Commission" (April 2006), http://ec.europa.eu/development/icenter/repository/eu_consensus_en.pdf (accessed January 2013).

6. See, for example, USAID's request for proposals (RfP) for a local governance project in Tajikistan. Solicitation Number: SOL-176-12-000002. Federal Business Opportunities, https://www.fbo.gov/index?s=opportunity &mode=form&id=81d933dcf93b8a05e92eb9fe8f2921e6&tab=core&_cview =1 (accessed January 2013).

7. Organisation Development, "Five Core Theories—Systems Theory—Organisation Development," sponsored by Fortitude Development Limited, http://organisationdevelopment.org/?p=218 or http://www.fortitudedevelopment.co.uk/ (accessed January 2103).

8. See, for example, James Dobbins, "Who Lost Iraq? Lessons from the Debacle," *Foreign Affairs* 86, no. 5 (September–October 2007): 61–74; Frank Ledwidge, *Losing Small Wars: British Military Failure in Iraq and Afghanistan* (New Haven, CT: Yale University Press, 2001); Ray Salvatore Jennings, *The Road Ahead: Lessons in Nation Building from Japan, Germany, and Afghanistan for Postwar Iraq,* Peaceworks no. 49 (Washington, DC: United States Institute of Peace, 2009).

9. World Bank, *World Development Report 2011: Conflict, Security, and Development* (Washington, DC: World Bank, 2011), 87.

10. Thomas E. Ricks, *Fiasco: The American Military Adventure in Iraq* (New York: Penguin, 2006), 175; US Army War College, Army Peacekeeping and Stability Operations Institute (PKSOI) and the United States Institute of Peace, *Guiding Principles for Stabilization and Reconstruction* (Washington, DC: United States Institute of Peace Press, 2009), 1–2.

11. Chester Crocker, "Peacemaking and Mediation: Dynamics of a Changing Field," Coping with Crisis Working Paper Series (New York: International Peace Academy, March 2007), foreword.

12. Peter Langseth, Office of Drug Control and Crime Prevention, United Nations Office at Vienna, "Prevention: An Effective Tool to Reduce Corruption," paper presented at the ISPAC conference "Responding to the Challenge of Corruption," November 19, 1999, Milan.

13. Gay Rosenblum-Kumar, Africa Region, *Capacity-Building in Conflict Management,* UNDP SPPD Document (May 2001), http://www.unpan.org/information/technical%20highlights/conflictpg.htm.

14. US Army, *Multi-Service Tactics, Techniques, and Procedures for Advising Foreign Forces,* FM 3-07/MCRP 3-33.8A/NTTP 3-07.5/AFTTP 3-2.76.

15. http://www.defense.gov/home/features/2011/0211_moda/.

16. John Saxby, *Local Ownership and Development Co-operation: The Role of Northern Civil Society,* Issues Paper (Ottawa: Canadian International Development Assistance, March 2003), http://www.ccic.ca/_files/en/what_we_do/002_aid_the_role_of_northern_civil_society.pdf.

17. Richard Caplan, "Partner or Patron? International Civil Administration and Local Capacity-Building," *International Peacekeeping* 11, no. 2 (2004).

18. Michael Szporluk, "A Framework for Understanding Accountability of International NGOs and Global Good Governance," *Indiana Journal of Global Legal Studies* 16, no. 339 (2009).

3

What Is a Strategic Adviser?

THE PRIMARY ROLE OF AN ADVISER IS THAT OF CAPACITY BUILDER, but as Chapter 2 has explained, capacity builders can come in many shapes and sizes. What sets advising apart from other forms of contemporary capacity building, in particular training and mentoring? What, exactly, does an adviser do—and, no less importantly, *not* do? How does an individual who has been recruited because of her technical expertise make the transition from "expert" to "adviser"? And what principles should always guide the work of an adviser? This chapter answers each of these questions.

What Distinguishes Advising from Mentoring and Training?

The terms *advising, mentoring,* and *training* are often used interchangeably. They are, however, distinct activities, and the failure to distinguish between them can confuse both internationals and locals involved in capacity-building missions. Each activity has its place in the spectrum of capacity-building activities, and blurring the differences between them not only risks confusion about the nature of each activity but also threatens to fuel misunderstandings about the capacity-building enterprise as a whole.

What Does an Adviser Do?

To understand how advising differs from mentoring and training it is necessary, of course, to first know what an adviser does. The essential characteristics of an adviser are:

- Is deployed on capacity-building missions by government agencies, regional organizations, and intergovernmental organizations.
- Is recruited from a military or a civilian agency within a government that is part of an international effort to build capacity in a transitional or postconflict state.
- Usually is a seasoned practitioner in fields such as logistics management, human resources, gender mainstreaming, contracting, and procurement, and has years of experience in solving problems, addressing issues, making compromises, and observing the challenges and impact of his own organization.
- Typically, is deployed either for very short but frequent trips or for extended stays of one to two years in country.
- Is deployed to assist a specific government institution (e.g., a ministry of defense or ministry of education).
- Often is deployed as part of a team of advisers tasked with helping the institution identify problems and solutions.
- Has a target audience of decisionmakers within the institution (or the government as a whole) or those individuals who influence the decisionmakers.
- Operates at the strategic level, offering advice that can contribute to the development of systems, processes, policies, and procedures that address the inadequacies of weak governmental institutions.
- Is assigned to a counterpart who is usually an official who runs a department (or otherwise has authority over staff and procedures) that has been identified as in need of reform or other changes.
- Works with the counterpart to identify gaps in capacity and weak links in systems and to develop sustainable solutions.
- Has an equal relationship with his counterpart, because both have something to offer and gain from the other.

• Has no executive function; role is limited to sharing advice rather than making decisions, to supporting rather than leading.

What Do Trainers and Mentors Do?

Whereas advisers work at the strategic level, mentors and trainers work at the operational level, helping build capacity in the field. They assist in the implementation of decisions, policies, and procedures—some or all of which the advisers may have helped to shape.

Once a specific policy or procedure has been adopted, a *trainer* will help others learn how to effectively implement the policy or procedure. A trainer's target audience is people who will be implementing specific policies or procedures. A trainer's relationship to these individuals will be more "unidirectional" than the adviser's relationship with her counterpart—in other words, whereas an international adviser and local counterpart will share knowledge and ideas, a trainer will focus on imparting knowledge on a given issue to locals. A trainer educates a group of individuals that are either interested in acquiring or required to acquire a set of skills on specific topics of importance to their agency, ministry, or organization. Trainers in transitional environments impart general conflict management skills such as how to be an active listener and how to facilitate dialogue between parties to a conflict, as well as more specialized skills such as principles of criminology and human rights for police officers, judges, and other justice-sector professionals.

The relationship between the trainer and the learner is generally conducted within classroom-like environments in which learning takes place outside the realm of the environment in which learners will practice their newly acquired skills, and is limited by the duration of the training program (programs typically last from two or three days to two weeks). The trainer will spend her time imparting lessons to the learner, and while she will discover a little about the learners and their environment, the trainer will probably have a very limited perspective on the challenges that the learner will face once outside the training program.

The adviser enjoys a longer relationship with his counterpart. Adviser missions typically last about nine months (although some returned advisers, including MoDA graduates, recommend that tours should last for as long as two years in order to improve continuity), a period long enough to allow for solid relationships between advisers and counterparts to be established. Furthermore, the relationship exists in the workplace, not in the classroom, enabling the adviser to gain a firsthand understanding of the conditions and challenges that the counterpart faces. This understanding is valuable because advising demands an appreciation of numerous facets of the counterpart's environment: institutional norms, institutional capacity, political mandates, political system, ability to incorporate international norms such as human rights and humanitarian law, and so forth.

Mentors are more akin to advisers than trainers in terms of the length of their relationships with counterparts, but mentoring and advising differ in other ways. Like a trainer but unlike an adviser, a *mentor* works with implementers. A mentor is a professional from a donor country who shadows local actors as they participate in efforts to make their governments more capable and more effective. His relationship with the counterpart is less unidirectional than that of a trainer, though not entirely equal. Mentors witness the application of new skills and guide the procedural changes that are required. A mentor uses his experience to guide a counterpart and assist him in performing tasks.

A mentor is embedded and thus accompanies his counterpart on operations or missions. Mentors offer suggestions in the field, and often in the heat of the moment, to local officials on how to act in ways that are consistent with new doctrines or procedures. For example, a mentor may provide guidance to a newly trained police officer on how to arrest a suspect in a way that complies with international human rights laws, to which the national government has just decided to subscribe.

In contrast, advisers generally do not accompany their counterparts on missions. Rather, the adviser-counterpart relationship exists on a more strategic level, whereby the adviser assists in the development of an organizational structure for the reforming or restructuring organization. In sum, mentors teach by reinforcing new lessons, practices, and procedures learned in training contexts, whereas advisers present several possibilities and together with the counterpart evaluate the desirability and viability of those options.

What Do Advisers, Mentors, and Trainers Have in Common?

Training, mentoring, and advising differ markedly in terms of the nature of the relationship between teacher and learner, and the scope of the involvement of the teacher in the learner's on-the-job application of new skills. Despite their differences, these three functions also share some important similarities. The most notable is that they are all forms of knowledge transfer. Indeed, their overall objectives are to enhance the ability to perform specific tasks more effectively. The process of developing an adequate approach to knowledge transfer is the same for advisers, mentors, and trainers: it begins with a sound and comprehensive assessment, an evaluation of the existing capacity, an understanding of the opportunities and challenges that should be considered, an understanding of the impact of the intervention that the transfer of knowledge represents for the targeted community, and the preparation of a workable plan.

A single individual cannot perform the tasks of an adviser, mentor, and trainer simultaneously, but those who do perform these functions stand to benefit from one another's experiences. The decisions made at the strategic level will influence the activities of those involved at the operational level, and the experiences gained during the implementation of these policies at the operational level will influence future decisions at the strategic level. Ideally, therefore, lessons learned will be shared, contributing to a continuous cycle of learning and adapting at all levels.

What Is the Skill Set of an Effective Adviser?

Effective advisers need an unusual skill set. This skill set is unusual not so much because of its breadth (though it is broad) as because it is made up of two parts that are not commonly found together. One part consists of technical expertise; the other, of the skills of a knowledge broker. Moreover, technical experts are accustomed to exercising authority and taking charge in their professional lives, but to be effective as advisers, they have to demonstrate technical expertise while behaving not as leaders but as supporters. The international donor system staffs interventions by recruiting practitioners whose expertise is relevant to the reform effort. For instance, in a rule of law mission, international donors seek to enlist police officers, judges, corrections officers, prosecutors, and so forth. This approach makes sense insofar as professional expertise is essential if an adviser is to identify options to consider in the development of new procedures and practices. But technical expertise alone is inadequate to the demands of an adviser's job.

Advising requires a supplemental array of knowledge and skills that revolve around how to transfer knowledge and how to be sensitive and mindful of the various dynamics at play in a foreign environment. These skills include the ability to navigate through an unfamiliar cultural and institutional environment, develop a professional rapport, solicit information, diagnose problems, and brainstorm solutions.

For example, a police officer has much to offer when it comes to sharing practices and procedures in investigating crimes, strengthening a case that is admissible in court, and arresting an alleged perpetrator while respecting civil and human rights. Similarly, a judge understands the laws of her own country and knows how to interpret them and to issue judgment and sentence. Such professional expertise can be a significant asset to reconstruction efforts—but only if it is deployed in the field in a manner that is appropriate to local needs, cultures, and institutions, and only if the expert recognizes that the laws and procedures that exist in her own country are unlikely to be found in the new context. After all, the police officer–turned–adviser will not practice her craft in a capacity-strengthening mission. The judge-turned-adviser will not interpret law once in mission. Instead, these professionals will act as information and knowledge brokers. Like any expert, they have to identify gaps and needs and then comb their experience for practices that might fit the context and contribute to systematic capacity-building efforts.

How to Transform a Technical Expert into an Adviser

Once recruited, most advisers need careful preparation before they are deployed in order to help them transform themselves from technical experts into effective advisers. There are six principal elements involved in the transformation from a "doer" to a supporter of change.

1. The most challenging shift is the transition from seasoned practitioner to supporter or helper. Practitioners are used to *practicing* their craft and implementing policies and decisions. A judge, for example, will interpret laws; police officers will enforce them; border guards will patrol and detain; and so forth. The adviser, however, no longer practices her craft or implements policies and decisions like she did at home. Instead, the adviser will be asked to use the experience she has gained over the years to help others carry out their tasks more effectively. The adviser will not be doing the task for her counterparts. Rather, in order to facilitate the transition from a doer to a supporter of change, the adviser needs to establish herself as a resource. Drawing on her expertise, skills, and other personal attributes, the adviser must encourage the counterpart to solicit assistance and request advice.

2. The adviser needs to make a shift from being a decisionmaker to having no formal authority, or having only perceived authority. Professionals, or "doers," are used to getting things done by making authoritative decisions. For example, a judge makes a decision in the courtroom based upon rules, practices, and discretion. The seasoned practitioner is used to enjoying the formal authority to delegate, make decisions, and manage the performance of the staff. Only occasionally will an adviser have the authority to move projects forward in order to meet specific goals. Most of the time, advisers will be expected to foster the development of desirable outcomes without any formal authority or decisionmaking power. In order to do this, advisers need to creatively employ a range of tools.

3. The adviser may sometimes encounter instances in which he is misperceived by locals to be in charge, and those locals may be eager to follow every proposal that the adviser makes. This is a precarious situation and is best avoided. It can usually be avoided by consulting with local counterparts as much as possible before proposing options. Advisers must bear in mind that they do not hold the key to all solutions.

4. Seasoned practitioners have professional reputations and are often sought after in their respective communities. In these environments, the professional's reputation makes it easier for him to get the job done, to get others on board, and to tap into the wider professional network. But in a foreign country, the adviser arrives with little or no reputation. An adviser will have to expend a significant amount of effort to establish a professional reputation, especially at the beginning of the tour. On the positive side, the absence of reputation means that the adviser does not have a negative reputation, and the counterpart may be keen to start working with the adviser. The adviser has an opportunity to make use of this situation to build a peer-to-peer relationship and foster a partnership of trust and confidence.

5. In some cases, however, the adviser arrives in country with a bad reputation, either because the adviser is tarnished by the existing poor reputation of his deploying country or institution, or because his predecessor's track record was poor, or for some other reason beyond his control. As was discussed previously, in such situations the adviser should try, patiently and diligently, to build a positive reputation.

6. When working in one's native country, working professionals are aware of office policies, institutional procedures and practices, and relevant cultural norms. They can thus navigate smoothly within the institutional hierarchy, display the appropriate work ethic, recognize the preferred tempo of the workplace, and otherwise avoid offending colleagues while nurturing their support and cooperation.

7. An adviser, by contrast, usually arrives in a country with little or no knowledge of the culture of the country or of the institution to which she is assigned. Some degree of cultural familiarity can be fostered before deployment through trainings and briefings, but a thorough understanding of the local culture can be acquired only during the deployment. Chapter 8 explains how to build a reliable cultural compass.

8. Like a foreign culture, a foreign language can also impede an adviser's ability to operate effectively. At home, the technical expert has the linguistic skills to engage in highly complex professional interactions, avoid misunderstandings, waltz diplomatically through office politics, and convey highly nuanced ideas. When the technical expert is deployed as an adviser in a country with a different language, these skills are severely downgraded.

9. Language training before deployment can help an adviser develop knowledge of basic greetings that can contribute to rapport building. However, advisers should guard against attempting to have complex professional interactions in a language they do not know well. The astute adviser will signal in the beginning of the relationship that his language skills are limited. Even advisers who are already familiar with the local language should not automatically assume or give the impression that they are entirely fluent in it. Chapter 8 discusses the challenge of language in greater depth.

10. Professionals are usually expected to communicate in close to real time. Ideas, issues, and results are typically conveyed at a fast pace, and responses to new messages and new information are similarly expected to be swift. The adviser, however, has to transform from someone who constantly voices opinions and takes prompt action into an active listener and strategic planner. Active listening entails asking specific questions that will lead the discussion toward the goal of attaining specific knowledge or understanding. It means listening for specific information rather than listening to what the interlocutor wishes to share.

11. The adviser needs to learn as much about the situation and the context as possible. This does not mean that he is just a quiet observer. Rather, active listening requires asking probing questions of many people. The answers to such questions give the adviser a wealth of information and opinions (including contradictory opinions) with which the adviser can make educated assessments about the needed capacity.

What Principles Should Guide the Work of an Adviser?

The main task of the adviser is to share expertise, and thus a vital part of the adviser's skill set is the ability to identify which elements of her expertise are most relevant to the foreign environment and which ideas are most likely to work within the local context.

An adviser must demonstrate to his counterpart, local staff, and other stakeholders that he understands the problems that have plagued reform efforts in the past. The adviser must resist the lure of simple solutions. There are no easy solutions. If there were, local actors would have already implemented them. An adviser who conveys this understanding to local actors will earn a reputation for humility and respect for colleagues while signaling that the supplementary assistance that the adviser can provide is needed due to the complexity of the situation.

Before sharing an idea, the adviser should see if it accords with four cardinal principles of capacity building: nurture local ownership; emphasize sustainability; do no harm; and demonstrate respect, empathy, and humility. These principles, which should always guide the work of an adviser, can be used as a series of filters to screen out unworkable, inapplicable, or unhelpful proposals. An idea that runs counter to one or more of the four principles requires some adjustment to fit the environment for which it is proposed. Even an idea that passes through each of the four filters will still likely need some modification, but at least it is probably environmentally sensitive and can thus be proposed with confidence.

Principle 1: Nurture Local Ownership

The concept of local ownership holds that local actors and constituencies should control the identification, design, and implementation of reform processes and the policies and procedures they generate. Local ownership is a principle that should guide the transition from crisis management to the reconstruction and/or development phase of the government.

Advisers will face various dilemmas in their mission as they relate to local ownership on both macro and micro levels. From a macro perspective, local ownership may appear to advisers to require a return to the "normal" that reigned prior to the conflict or the political transition now under way. Advisers, however, should be wary of this oversimplification of the reconstruction dynamic. In most cases, it is imperative to distinguish between the "old normal" and the "new normal." After all, the old order may well have contributed to the conflict or precipitated its own demise. Furthermore, traditional power structures are often in conflict with universal principles, such as human rights, that reform operations seek to integrate into a post-conflict or transitional country's political and legal systems. Therefore, a "new normal" is usually preferable, albeit one that retains those elements that functioned effectively and equitably in the old.

Capacity strengthening should work toward creating this "new normal" with local actors at the helm. In the absence of local ownership, the "new normal" may end up consisting of unsuitable or unsustainable institutions that protect nontransparent political, judicial, and financial processes.

The implementation of local ownership requires a keen understanding of the local actors and their interests, positions, goals, and plans. There are three types of local actors who can represent entry points for the adviser wishing to respect the local ownership principle: (1) the population in both organized and unorganized forms, including citizens, civil society (including the media and professional organizations), and the business community; (2) the authorities, including the political leadership, civil servants, and local government officials; and (3) actors in the reform and reconstruction sector.

However, eager advisers who want to reach out to these groups and infuse local ownership into their programs and projects may quickly find themselves frustrated. The transition to local ownership is a gradual process. To be sure, the goal is for local actors to retain or regain the maximum amount of authority over reconstruction efforts as soon as possible. Capacity, however, is highly dependent on local competence, resources, and political and social local context. Hence, the effective adviser works diligently to promote the gradual development of the competences necessary for institutions and their staffs to provide services (e.g., public order, law enforcement, defense, education, healthcare, transportation). Nurturing local

Why Internationals Find It Hard to Foster Local Ownership

International actors may assert their allegiance to the concept of local ownership, but in the field "local ownership" means merely securing local buy-in for a predetermined international agenda or adjusting predesigned international policies so that they can be implemented by local structures.

This tendency to impose predefined policies rather than to let locals determine their own solutions is exacerbated by the fact that most daily interactions between external and internal actors are dominated by an asymmetric relationship in favor of the internationals. The failure to encourage local autonomy is also made worse by a lack of intercultural skills and an unwillingness to learn on the part of the international staff.

ideas and solutions also increases the chances that reform and change will enjoy popular and political acceptance and buy-in from both implementers and end users of a service.

Local ownership should not be glorified. Local actors cannot easily be transformed into ardent and effective champions of reform. Advisers commonly encounter two major problems as they seek to nurture local ownership of their projects. The first is the extent to which local actors are willing to conduct a reform process. The second is the extent to which local actors are able to contribute to the reform efforts. Fortunately, a variety of mechanisms exist with which to tackle these problems, including consultations, shared authority (e.g., interim governments and hybrid agencies that are staffed by both internationals and locals), and the inclusion of professionals from the country in transition.

More generally, efforts to foster local ownership should be conducted with the following principles in mind:

- Make all actions highly transparent.
- Allocate resources and communicate reform efforts to the population to elicit their trust in government institutions.
- Develop the ability of institutions to systematically, equitably, and reliably deliver the services they were created to provide.
- Listen to local actors, stakeholders, and counterparts; ask them about their concerns; show respect for their views; and keep an open mind about the needs they perceive and the solutions they recommend.

Principle 2: Emphasize Sustainability

The goal of an international mission should be to create capacity that will remain in place and continue to be effective after the intervener departs.

The concept of sustainability was popularized in the context of development and environmental protection, but it has become a key part of the desired approach to capacity-building activities and is closely linked to activities such as training, teaching, mentoring, and advising. Broadly speaking, sustainability refers to the ability to maintain either a state or a process. In the field of environmental protection, a sustainable system requires a collective effort to utilize resources (human and capital) within a zone that can be maintained. In 1989, the World Commission on Environment and Development articulated the following definition of sustainability, which has become widely accepted: "[to meet] the needs of the present without compromising the ability of future generations to meet their own needs."[1]

In capacity-building missions, sustainability is often dependent on the extent to which local ideas for solutions influence the formulation of the new normal. Furthermore, the quest for sustainability is complex and is marked by myriad dilemmas between addressing short-term obstacles to peace (such as the lack of security) and long-term challenges (such as strengthening the capacity of the local institutions to deliver services, enact laws, and promulgate regulations). A process that is sustainable is one that resolves such conflicts between various competing goals and seeks the simultaneous pursuit of economic prosperity, environmental quality, and social equity.

Sustainable processes can only be established and maintained if the actors involved in those processes are aware of the need for sustainability. Ensuring sustainability is a high-maintenance and continuous effort in which resources must be efficiently deployed with a long-term view.

Evaluations are essential to analyze and gauge the effectiveness of the process, to inform the redesign of the project, and to assess the impact of the work on the targeted populations. There are two types of evaluations that should both be conducted on a regular basis. First, a "process evaluation" allows one to identify the limitations encountered due to poor or inefficient resource allocation. Second, an "impact evaluation" seeks to assess the adequacy of the project, its content, and its delivery method to measure it against project goals.

Chapter 10 discusses sustainability in greater depth.

Principle 3: Do No Harm

"Do no harm" was broadened from a medical imperative to a social imperative by Mary B. Anderson in her 1999 book of the same name, which called for a redesign of development assistance programs so that they would do no harm while doing their intended good.[2] Do no harm is a maxim that acknowledges that any intervention carries with it the risk of doing more harm than good. Practitioners should proceed with programs only after careful consideration and widespread consultation. In assistance activities, the maxim recognizes that resources inevitably represent the distribution of power and wealth and will create tensions if careful attention is not given to how they are distributed. The concept also applies to institutions that share the same space in an intervention. Even if there is no imperative to coordinate or work together, institutions in the field should be sensitive to the activities of others and not undercut or undermine them.

In any capacity-building arena, the principle of do no harm acknowledges that some actions, although well intended, can carry unforeseen negative consequences. Advisers should implement ideas only after first deliberating carefully and consulting widely. For example, an adviser might initially decide to recommend that an official be replaced because he is corrupt and threatens the financial viability of the institution, but on closer consideration may recognize that ousting the official may upset a precarious balance between ethnic groups within the institution and endanger the institution's stability. In this instance, the adviser must understand his environment well enough and have listened to his counterpart long enough to understand the ramifications of such a recommendation. (In doing so, the advisers will employ a variety of skills discussed in later chapters, including strategic listening, facilitation of dialogue, establishing a peer-to-peer relationship, and seeing the counterpart as a cultural adviser.) The adviser must see it as a responsibility to test a new idea for unintended consequences, direct or indirect.

To take another example: Dismissing from service soldiers who have deserted their duty would make a defense ministry more efficient, because pay would be reserved for those soldiers who are present and willing to go out on operations. But dealing with this problem head-on may have devastating consequences. The adviser may discover that removing soldiers who have deserted from payrolls would mean depriving people of their only source of income. If they can find no alternative employment, they may resort to violence, thereby increasing the level of insecurity and exerting additional pressure on an already overstretched police service. This does not mean that the adviser should ignore the problem of paying deserters, but it does mean that the adviser must be vigilant about the possible negative consequences of any new approach and identify strategies to mitigate risks.

Advisers should first reflect by themselves on the viability of a recommendation in terms both of budgets and of the competence of the staff and other relevant stakeholders. This reflection will likely involve the formulation of questions for various actors, the answers to which may reveal valuable information to be used in the identification of viable solutions. A viable solution is one that is sustainable from feasibility and financial standpoints and that is seen as adequate by local actors, implementers, and end users (i.e., the public).

Principle 4: Demonstrate Respect, Empathy, and Humility

Every piece of advice that the adviser offers must be presented with respect, empathy, and humility. These three qualities form a foundation on which the adviser can build a productive relationship with counterparts and relevant stakeholders. These qualities must be evident in the adviser's behavior from the very first steps in building a relationship with a new counterpart, and must continue to be displayed throughout all phases of the advising relationship.

The absence of just one of these qualities could severely impair advising activities and effectiveness, or even jeopardize a mission. By the same token, their embrace is likely to contribute greatly to building trust and enduring relationships. Indeed, without some degree of trust in a relationship, any advice will be rejected or at least regarded skeptically. It is important to note, however, that while establishing trust must be a constant goal, trust is not a tool, and establishing trust is not a skill in itself; it takes a complex web of skills to build trust.

Respect. Respect is relevant in two ways. First, the adviser should act in a respectful manner toward the people she encounters, including showing respect for their work, their level of competence (even if that is below the standard to which the adviser is accustomed), and their overall ability to work within a variety of constraints while seeking to meet their daily goals. The adviser displays respect by striving to learn and understand in a manner that recognizes and acknowledges the achievements and capabilities displayed by local actors.

Second, an adviser should respect the existing system and level of capacity. The effective adviser shows respect for what exists, and understands why it exists as it does, why it does not contain certain elements, and how it does or does not address problems. Respecting the systems that exist shows that the adviser understands the difficulties of reform. In cases where "good enough" is not in fact good enough, advisers have an opportunity to fill the gaps. However, it is crucial to show interest in and incorporate what already works and to build on it where necessary to develop greater capacity.

No one enjoys listening to an outsider suggest that a procedure crafted and implemented by a hard-working group of individuals is worthless and should be thrown away. That dislike is accentuated when the outsider evidently has little understanding of the local context and a very limited appreciation of the multitude of local obstacles.

To offer an example: An adviser working on the procurement systems of a ministry identifies a procedure that entails getting thirteen signatures before the contracting process takes place. The adviser, who has procurement experience, recommends that the entire procedure be canceled and a new one adopted that requires the authorization of only three individuals closely tied to the procurement process. What the adviser does not know, however, is that the thirteen-signature process had been put in place over time to combat corrupt practices. For this environment, at the time it was introduced, the thirteen-signature process was the right approach. The adviser's recommendation to reduce the number of authorizations to three may open the door for corruption to reenter the system. The adviser was correct in suggesting that the existing procedure was slowing down the process and could cripple the operations supported by the ministry. However, understanding the history of the current practice would have given the adviser the insight needed to reduce lead times for procurement while maintaining the necessary safeguards. It may be that at the time the policy was formulated, the thirteen signatures were necessary because of the make-up of the staff and the absence of other relevant procedures. It may be that the process could now be streamlined while still maintaining the level of control necessary to address corrupt practices. Only sustained observation and active listening will tell.

Empathy. An adviser also needs to display empathy. However, it is important to distinguish between sympathy and empathy. Sympathy is simply feeling sorry for someone; empathy is the ability to imagine how someone feels. Advisers usually work with individuals who have experienced violent conflict and intense fear. Advisers should not express sympathy or pity for their counterpart (pity is likely to be unwelcome) or explicitly quiz their counterpart about his traumatic experience (which is likely to cause some distress), but neither should they completely ignore the counterpart's experience of conflict. An adviser must have the ability to understand people in their context and see the environment through their eyes; such understanding will be greatly appreciated and will help to establish the human element of the professional relationship with counterparts. A high degree of implied empathy in the words that an adviser chooses and even the ideas that he puts forward will help the counterpart to feel understood and respected and to become more receptive to outside support.

Most advisers from donor countries have not themselves endured years of violence, war, loss, and subsequent trauma. Such experiences do leave traumatic legacies, but they can also leave individuals wiser about their environment, tougher in facing up to its challenges, and more imaginative about how to improve it. Advisers should not be blind to the fact that their counterparts may have learned useful lessons from experiences that the advisers have not undergone.

Humility. Advisers must be humble in the way they approach their entire project. They must understand that they are in a foreign environment riddled with unknowns and subtleties that outsiders will likely miss, even though they are important to the development of a productive professional relationship with local actors. A humble adviser is modest because she understands that she is an information broker, not the source of infallible ideas for plugging gaps in capacity. Advisers also show humility by frequently referring to the counterpart's assessment and seeking the advice of the counterpart on what information is needed.

Humility lies in the understanding that while an expert knows about her home system, the ideas she presents are only potential solutions that must be adapted to the local context, a task best left to the counterpart and his superiors. Advisers are outsiders and hence seldom well placed to assess the viability of a specific system or approach and the likelihood of buy-in by staffs, institutions, and the general public. Good advisers bear in mind that the system in which they operate at home also is imperfect, and they explain both the pros and cons of their ideas.

Humility also involves acknowledging to the counterpart and any other interlocutors that the adviser needs help to navigate the cultural, historical, and linguistic landscape—help that only local actors can provide.

Being humble is no small feat for individuals who have acquired significant expertise in their professional lives, have had to show results, and whose home environments are comfortable, familiar, and receptive to change. It is tempting to emphasize the successes of one's own systems, but it is best to keep in mind that the experience being shared may not be relevant and that the adviser's frame of reference may not apply. Being humble allows the adviser to refrain from making quick analogies and importing ready-made solutions. The history of peacebuilding has shown that the best results stem from a partnership between the outside expert and the local counterpart.[3] This is otherwise known as the lesson that "cookie-cutter solutions don't export."

Applying the Principles

When an adviser identifies a particular idea for a new approach, policy, or procedure, the adviser should ask herself a number of questions that will help in assessing the viability of the idea and determining how to mitigate its possible negative consequences.

1. *Nurture Local Ownership*

How was the idea identified? Whose feedback was solicited and what was learned in the process? Is the idea shaped by the context described by local actors?

Which components of the idea are foreign to me?

Which aspects are locally defined and locally derived problems and solutions?

Overall: Does the idea incorporate local concerns and ideas?

2. *Emphasize Sustainability*

Do the staff who have to institutionalize (i.e., implement and maintain) the system that would result from the implementation of the idea have the necessary competences and skills? Are those skills readily found in the local society or can they at least be taught to staff members?

Have the counterpart, staff, or other local actors bought in to the idea, and do they fully understand what will be required to implement it? Can someone sell the idea without my help?

Is this idea viable in terms of available resources: financial, material, educational, and so forth?

Overall: Is the procedure and/or system that will result from implementation of this idea going to be maintained, safeguarded, and even updated after the advising mission (or just the adviser) leaves?

3. *Do No Harm*
Which populations will be impacted by the change? How?

What could be the negative consequences? Which segments of the population will they affect? How?

Who will likely be the losers as a result of the implementation? How will they react and why?

Who will benefit? Can they use what they gain to harm others?

Overall: How can the vetting of an idea be integrated into the new approach and used to make the idea more beneficial and less costly?

4. *Demonstrate Respect, Empathy, and Humility*
Is the idea heavily reliant on my practices and procedures back at home?

To what extent do I really understand the constraints and challenges that this idea will face? Am I merely *assuming* that I understand?

Is this idea building on or filling gaps in the existing system? Or is this idea one that creates a blank slate, sending the signal that there are no effective mechanisms worth keeping?

Is the idea insulting or counterintuitive to the history, conflict environment, and/or personal trauma of those who have to implement this idea? Does this idea respect the limitations of those who have to sell or defend the resulting procedures?

Overall: Would the approach offend many people or disregard components of existing systems that should be incorporated or be used as the foundation for reform? In other words, does the approach build on existing systems that have been deemed to be at least partly effective?

Notes

1. United Nations General Assembly, "Report on the World Commission on Environment and Development," Resolution A/RES/42/187 (December 11, 1987).

2. Mary B. Anderson, *Do No Harm: How Aid Can Support Peace—or War* (Boulder, CO: Lynne Rienner, 1999).

3. A. Heather Coyne, *Empowering Local Peacebuilders: Strategies for Effective Engagement of Local Actors in Peace Operations*, Building Peace no. 2 (Washington, DC: United States Institute of Peace, March 2012), http://www.usip.org/publications/empowering-local-peacebuilders.

4

Coping with Challenges

ADHERING TO THE GENERAL PRINCIPLES LAID OUT IN CHAPTER 3 will help an adviser stay on the right road, using his skill set and training to drive steadily toward the mission's goal instead of taking a wrong turn or plunging off the side of the highway because of a catastrophic neglect of local conditions. But what does an adviser do when he hits a bump in the road or runs into a major roadblock?

This chapter describes the kinds of obstacles that an adviser is likely to encounter from the very outset of his deployment and offers guidance on how to navigate safely around them. It groups those obstacles into two distinct yet often interdependent categories— expectations and dilemmas—and explains the importance of keeping expectations realistic and navigating dilemmas carefully. The chapter then looks at the challenges an adviser faces in securing institutional buy-in for strategies and solutions intended to build capacity, and in establishing his authority, credibility, and legitimacy. An adviser has to start tackling these twin challenges from the start of the mission, but he should never assume that either challenge has been met and can henceforth be ignored. Like steering a car, both require constant attention, a clear sense of direction, and a light touch.

Have Realistic Expectations

Advisers must try to be realistic about what they can achieve during their mission. Otherwise, they risk finding themselves highly frus-

The Challenges Facing an Adviser: A Typical Scenario

Aside from running into unexpected obstacles, what sorts of "ordinary" challenges is an adviser likely to encounter? The following scenario offers a realistic example of the kinds of problems that are part and parcel of an adviser's job.

* * *

Country X, which is transitioning from authoritarian rule to democracy, is hosting an international intervention. A US Air Force officer is assigned to serve as senior adviser to the Foreign Relations Department in Country X's Ministry of Interior at the request of the multinational command leading the intervention. The officer's mandate is to advise the minister on how to build the Foreign Relations Department to facilitate and manage the cooperation between the ministry and donors, specifically militaries of the coalition. The adviser's specific duties include:

- Helping to create and implement standardized procedures for managing donations of equipment and training.
- Systematizing the interaction between the ministry, the multinational command, and its member countries to improve the ministry's ability to accept donations of police equipment and training in the use of that equipment.
- Advising the Foreign Relations Department on how to develop the capability to administer and manage donations of funds, equipment, and training.

The adviser quickly encounters several obstacles. The Foreign Relations Department turns out to be irrelevant to managing donations, because donor relations are controlled by the Office of the Minister and by a deputy minister. That office also sets policy and determines the role of the Foreign Relations Department. In terms of the personalities involved, the adviser finds reason for both optimism and pessimism about accomplishing his assignment. On the bright side, the minister believes that the Foreign Relations Department should handle cooperation with the military and donations of equipment; on the gloomy side, the minister believes it should do so only if it reports directly to his office and only if his chief of staff participates in the process.

The deputy minister, who has been the main contributor to the development of a system to manage donations, believes that managing and soliciting donations of equipment is too important to leave to anyone but the people in his office. The deputy minister has had advisers in the past who disrespected the systems already in place; not surprisingly, he has lost faith in the idea of getting guidance and support from international advisers. Meanwhile, donors have provided equipment for several months but are becoming disillusioned by the lack of response to their requests for information on how the equipment is being distributed, used, and maintained, and on how individuals are being trained to use it.

Past advisers tried to shoulder the burden of managing donations themselves, but in doing so left the department's staff inexperienced in the day-to-day management of operations and relations with the military. The staff has limited management experience generally and no experience of restructuring procedures and practices. To make the new adviser's task yet more daunting, training is unpopular among both upper and lower ranks of the staff.

In short, the adviser faces an array of formidable challenges:

- Sharing expertise that has to fit in a foreign environment.
- Supporting the development of plans and implementation activities in a system with dynamics with which the adviser is unfamiliar.
- Working with staff with limited experience in key areas.
- Coordinating with other international actors.
- Suggesting change when the appetite for change is modest or nonexistent.
- Overcoming the poor reputation that past advisers have earned.

trated and largely ineffective. For instance, when an adviser wrongly assumes that her counterpart possesses specific technical knowledge or understanding of information, or when the adviser mistakenly anticipates a willing attitude toward learning, disillusionment is likely to follow, which will make the adviser less energetic and more likely to misperceive local attitudes and realities, seeing the situation as bleaker than it actually is.

To forestall this danger, advisers must develop realistic expectations about all aspects of their missions: coordination, communication, resource allocation, political navigation, and even their own limitations when faced with insecurity, high stress, and high levels of unpredictability and frustration. Advisers must also be realistic about time: the goals that advisers set for themselves and for the targets of their capacity-building endeavors must be achievable within the time available—that is, within the period during which the adviser is deployed or otherwise involved in the project.

If it does not already exist, this sense of realism should begin to develop when the adviser assesses the conflict and the reform effort, and comes to recognize she has very little understanding of the modus operandi and/or attitudes of local actors. Indeed, the adviser should not only keep her own expectations realistic but also recognize those expectations are not the same as those of her counterpart—nor, indeed, necessarily the same as those of her colleagues and bosses. Reform efforts typically require significant collaboration, cooperation, and compromise involving many actors (as discussed in detail in Chapter 9). Those actors differ not only in terms of their positions, goals, and interests but also their perceptions and worldviews. Expectations are tightly connected to assumptions about the way the world works, and thus diverging worldviews tend to yield diverging perspectives.

The risk of harboring inflated or misguided motives is not confined to advisers. Indeed, entire capacity-building missions have had unrealistic goals and have tried to appease all people and all problems instead of prioritizing objectives. The phrase "Afghan good enough"[1] encapsulates a very important lesson that the international community learned in Afghanistan: namely, that a workable solution is a good solution, no matter how unsophisticated or unusual it may look to Western eyes. What matters is whether the approach adopted helps the institution perform more effectively and deliver better services. The international community's experience in Afghanistan—and elsewhere—points clearly to the fact that it is much better to have a simple, effective system than one that has lots of finely calibrated components but that is never going to be used.

Too often, international interventions aim to introduce perfect solutions—solutions that have not yet become a reality even in the most stable countries or environments. This is a natural tendency, wanting to help societies that have suffered dreadfully leapfrog over problems and speedily reach an Olympian level of institutional efficiency and social equitability. However, aspiring to an illusory ideal does no one any favors, least of all a postconflict or transitional society that needs to tackle its problems and to develop solutions that, for all their imperfections, work within the local environment.

Essentially, the adviser must recognize that her sphere of potential impact is actually quite small. As depicted in Figure 4.1, the adviser has a finite range of room in which to operate. Effective advisers identify this space and do not seek to work outside of it. It is futile for an adviser to try to change the international system or the current mission, or strive to alter the interests and positions of local actors. Change, if it comes, will be incremental and highly localized, and it will result from the adviser and her counterpart working together to discover new ideas and old problems.

Figure 4.1 An Adviser's Sphere of Potential Impact

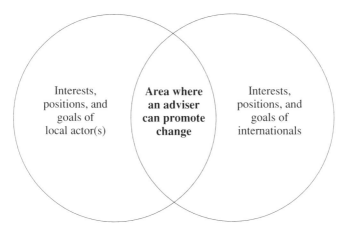

Many dynamics constrain an adviser's sphere of potential impact. Some constraints are very concrete in nature. For instance, because of security concerns in very hostile environments, an adviser may not be able to travel in person to meet a counterpart and may instead have to rely on telephone communication. Needless to say, phone conversations can be a highly problematic means of conducting capacity-building activities between professionals who have different cultures, language, assumptions, perceptions, and expectations. Other constraints are less prosaic. For example, the sheer scale and complexity of an international operation can limit an adviser's access to a counterpart, which of course greatly complicates the task of identifying and reducing gaps in capacity. Different organizational cultures (such as those of the military and civilian agencies), different funding rules, different approaches to governance reform: all such factors work together to limit the adviser's sphere.

Navigate Dilemmas

A dilemma is a fork in the road that requires a traveler to choose which one of the two directions to take. Each direction is an imperfect choice that will have consequences. Advisers can expect to face many dilemmas as they carry out capacity-building activities. Indeed, the context in which capacity-building activities takes place is riddled with uncertainty and imperfect decisions. Advisers support change, and change is a process of advancing from one fork in the road to another and then to another—and so on, with imperfections and consequences accumulating in unpredictable ways.

How one addresses a dilemma is a highly personal choice that is usually determined by an individual's tolerance for risk and understanding of the situation. Faced with the same dilemma, ten advisers might respond in ten different ways, depending on each adviser's interpersonal style, rank, skill set, knowledge, and assessment of the specific attributes of the situation on the ground and the overall goals of the mission.

The most important aspect of dealing with dilemmas is to avoid surprise when they arise. They add stress to an already uncertain situation, especially at the beginning of a project or mission. But if an adviser anticipates that various and even competing interests will inevitably surface, he will be better prepared to evaluate the issues and interests at stake in each specific case. Understanding where and why those competing interests diverge and where they might actually converge will help the adviser to plan the best course of action.

Among the numerous dilemmas that advisers may encounter, seven types are very common:

- International bosses vs. local bosses
- Sustainability vs. dependency
- Inaction vs. co-optation
- Service delivery in the short term vs. institutional strengthening
- International ethics vs. existing practices
- Trust vs. security
- Intrusive planning vs. no planning

International vs. Local Bosses

Advisers have multiple bosses, all of whom have different interests, positions, perceptions, missions, caveats, and modus operandi. Significant challenges arise when these bosses' goals and interests differ, diverge, or clash.

An adviser is required to answer to at least three different authorities. In the first place, the adviser is expected to report to her deploying government agency or donor institution (or sometimes an NGO) that provides the adviser with the financial and managerial support she requires for the mission. Second, the adviser is likely to be a part of a larger mission, either within a country team (an embassy or other diplomatic mission, for example) or as part of a multilateral mission (a UN, EU, or North Atlantic Treaty Organization [NATO] mission, for example). These missions require the adviser to function within their guidelines and adhere to specific rules of engagement and reporting mechanisms. Third, the adviser has a local counterpart who works for an institution that is the focus of the adviser's capacity-building task; the adviser has certain obligations toward that counterpart and that institution.

Almost inevitably, these authorities may sometimes give the adviser conflicting instructions or have differing expectations of the adviser's priorities. The adviser must be able to recognize this situation and decide on a case-by-case basis which task to prioritize at a given time. Having a clear idea about one's mandate and mission, from the early stages of a mission onward, can help an adviser define priorities.

Sustainability vs. Dependency

Establishing sustainable local structures and capacities requires a long-term external commitment of resources and other forms of support. Yet, local institutions that receive long-term international assistance tend to become dependent on it.

Advisers can try to find a middle path between sustainability and dependency by sharing knowledge, ideas, and solutions that do not require enduring international support and can instead be funded and/or supported by the host government's or institution's budget. The adviser should think creatively and consult with his local counterpart to identify a strategy that balances the building of local capacity with the weaning away of international funds. Care has to be taken not to pull away the funding too soon in case doing so would result in a collapse of a nascent and still very fragile system. A key challenge is to determine when is the earliest, yet most appropriate, time for the transition to local capacity to take place.

Inaction vs. Co-optation

Co-optation has several meanings, and perhaps the most common one is to neutralize opposition by assimilating an opponent into one's own system or culture. In the field of advising, however, "co-optation" usually entails appropriating for oneself the authority to decide what changes to make. Advisers are very likely to identify some areas in which a change in a procedure or system seems highly desirable. However, advisers must resist at all times the temptation to give themselves the authority to make those changes happen. Why? Because the adviser, who is an outsider, will seldom be able to figure out how to make a change stick; local dynamics, actors, and interests will almost always undermine any change imposed from outside. While moving forward may seem impossible to the adviser unless he grabs the reins of authority, the adviser should instead encourage counterparts and stakeholders to discuss an issue as long and often as they need to in order to arrive at a joint decision about how best to move forward.

Advisers do not have the authority to impose change; their role is to share ideas about how to address problems. This understanding of the role of the adviser, it should be noted, does not always square with the mandate of the larger mission or match how the adviser's bosses and counterparts conceptualize capacity building. Against such a background, and with great pressure on the adviser to demonstrate that she is "getting the job done," it can be extremely difficult for an adviser to resist the temptation to co-opt authority or coerce a counterpart. Nonetheless, an adviser who wishes to be effective must remain a resource for a decisionmaker, rather than becoming a decisionmaker herself. The appropriate course to take is to submit a proposal to a counterpart, who will then decide to act on that proposal, refine it, or reject it. The effective adviser does all that is possible to move a project along by supporting gradual shifts in modus operandi without bypassing those with formal authority.

Service Delivery in the Short Term vs. Institutional Strengthening

When a host government institution lacks the capacity to deliver services to its target population, an adviser may be tempted to tap the resources of the international mission to accomplish the task at hand. For example, if riots take place and the police or the military do not respond or have responded inadequately in the past, advisers in ministries may consider recommending that international military or police units step in.

This option, however, should be kept as a last resort. Solutions that rely on international actors and capacities are not long-term solutions and tend to undermine the development of local capacity. Whenever possible, an adviser should seek out the collaboration of local actors, support local leadership, and seek to promote the development of processes that will encourage the delivery of services reliably and consistently. For instance, if riots are anticipated, the adviser might suggest the creation of joint patrols of local and international security personnel, so that the capacities of the former can be built with the support of the latter.

Before making a decision to step in and intervene in a way that will build no capacity, the effective adviser weighs the cost of inaction against the consequences of involvement. In some cases, it is better to allow a service not to be delivered, even though its absence may cause significant hardship, than to step in and use international resources to get the job done. Fostering dependency on a temporary resource will not address the root cause of the problem.

Having said that, sometimes a long-term perspective can be misleading. Some short-term problems can be tolerated, but others may pose an existential threat to the mission or the institution in which the adviser is working. There is no sense in letting a government fail to deliver a service today if that means the government will be fatally weakened tomorrow. For example, if the local police are expected to control a growing crowd, but have neither the equipment nor the training nor rules of engagement to handle such a situation, they will likely not enter the scene. The crowd may then get out of hand, lawlessness may spread across a city or region, and the government will be seen as too weak to maintain security. This impression may then be confirmed if the government eventually has to call on international troops to restore law and order. As a consequence, the fragile legitimacy of the government may be entirely demolished and months of work by the international community to bolster that government and that legitimacy will have been wasted. In some instances, long-term solutions are too long term. In such a case, an effective adviser looks to balance the long-term goal of capacity building with the short-term need to deliver a particular service.

International Ethics vs. Existing Practices

Advisers encounter many situations that challenge the code of ethics of the mission, the international community, or the adviser personally. Local practices may seem to violate these ethical codes, and after checking the specific guidelines and laws surrounding a particular issue, advisers are likely to find themselves deliberating ethics. Up to what point do you have to tolerate corrupt practices? Do you have to tolerate them at all? What do you do when you discover a corrupt practice?

These questions are rarely easy to answer. For example, an adviser may discover that funds dedicated to a specific project are being paid into a private account, where some of the funding disappears or is otherwise unaccounted for. However, the project in question is successful in terms of effectively addressing a problem in a given community. Should the adviser try to terminate the project because it is riddled with corruption, or should the adviser turn a blind eye toward the corruption because the project works?

At such times, an adviser should of course consult any pertinent rules and legal provisions. But he should also ask himself the following kinds of questions to help decide which, inevitably imperfect, option to take: What are the applicable policies and procedures for addressing corrupt practices? How widespread is the corruption in general in the country or the institution in question? What is the nature of the corrupt practice? How many people does the activity and/or practice involve? Has it been going on for long? Is this a recurring or a one-off practice? What are the underlying reasons for this practice (e.g., low or unpaid salaries, personal gain, or maintenance of standards of living)?

Trust vs. Security

The development of trust between an adviser and her counterparts is essential to the success of an adviser's mission. But if trust is to grow, the adviser needs access to the counterpart, and sometimes personal security considerations and policies significantly impair access.

Traveling to a ministry can be difficult in very hostile environments. Advisers have experienced lock-downs for prolonged periods during which they have been unable to meet with their counterparts. This can be a problem for counterparts, who may have to stop working, at least temporarily, on those projects that they have been developing jointly with their advisers. It can also send the message to counterparts and other local actors that the environment is too hostile for advisers—but not for locals. In other cases—as in Afghanistan in the wake of "blue-on-green attacks" (attacks by Afghan security forces on international forces)—advisers have been forced to carry weapons or have personal security guards. None of these security precautions is conducive to cultivating a direct and trusting relationship between local actors and internationals.

Access to local actors is not limited solely by considerations about the adviser's security. To the contrary, the locals themselves may deliberately limit their accessibility. Local officials may be too busy to want to make room in their hectic schedules for meetings with advisers, especially if the officials are skeptical of the role and

value of foreign advisers. Officials may also be wary of outside inter-
ference in their work. This occurs mostly because counterparts and
other ministry officials do not believe that outsiders understand the
local culture, history, and overall context, so they see little or no
value in the adviser's knowledge, essentially dismissing it as not
adaptable to the local environment.

Intrusive Planning vs. No Planning

Advisers who want to develop a plan to implement a proposed solution have two options. The first is for the adviser to draft a plan and
to submit it to the counterpart for his approval. The second option is
for the adviser to suggest that a plan would be a useful tool to transform the proposal into a functioning program and that she will assist
in the development of a strategy and plan. If the first option is taken,
the adviser will fail to build the capacity of the counterpart to
develop plans. Furthermore, the adviser will likely draft a plan that
omits components and mechanisms that are necessary in the local
context; such a plan will not create suitable and sustainable solutions. Overly intrusive plans and decisionmaking by external actors
tend to alienate local stakeholders (staff, users of the services,
providers of services to the agency), especially stakeholders who
will have to alter their behavior if the plans are implemented. If the
adviser opts for the second option, she will empower the counterpart
to take the reins of planning: identifying the resources to mobilize,
determining how to do so and who to bring into the process, deciding how to mitigate against potential challenges by framing the solution and its implementation in a manner that appeals to colleagues,
and so forth.

Which of these two options to take seems obvious—except for
the fact that the concept and activity of strategic planning, while very
important, are rarely part of the institutional culture in transitional
societies. It is common for counterparts to tell advisers that planning
is not part of the way things are done in their institutions. The very
idea of a strategic plan (i.e., a plan that establishes what needs to be
changed, how it is to be changed, when, with what resources, etc.) is
alien to most counterparts because the concept is one that only exists
in highly structured and complex organizations that espouse transparency, external oversight, and institution-wide procedures.

The adviser thus encounters a difficult dilemma: design and deliver a plan oneself or wait for a plan or a planning process that may never materialize. And waiting may leave the stabilization and transitional process to drift or stall.

Faced with this situation, advisers should do all they can to encourage the counterpart to start drafting a plan. For instance, an adviser could support a counterpart by asking the kinds of questions that have to be answered if a plan is to be developed. In practice, however, the adviser may need to step in and draft the plan herself. If this step has to be taken, it should be done with as light a touch as possible, ensuring that the counterpart is directly involved in the process. The adviser must avoid delivering a finished plan and should ask the counterpart to participate in the drafting and review of the plan by thinking through alternatives. Essentially, the adviser should teach by example.

Securing Institutional Buy-In

While the immediate targets for knowledge transfer are the counterparts and staff members who are expected to enhance capacity in specific ways, advisers must also aim at securing the buy-in of entire government institutions into a different way of operating. Capacity-building activities almost always involve one or more institutions in the governance structure. Even if capacity-strengthening efforts focus on civil society, civil society organizations are themselves promoters of a more capable governance structure.

An adviser must be mindful of the capacity of the institution he is endeavoring to help. While one cannot assume that all institutions have the political will to embrace reform, many institutions that receive assistance from donor states do accept that capacity-strengthening activities make them function more effectively. This limited level of buy-in for reform activity, however, is far too low for a successful transfer of knowledge to take place between the adviser and his counterpart. Knowledge transfer is a process that requires a significant commitment on the part of an institution's staff to acquiring new knowledge and/or skills and to altering mind-sets and practices.

An adviser whose mission it is to strengthen the capacity of a key institution should begin capacity-building activities by assessing the extent to which the institution is oriented toward reform and change.

Once the adviser has pinpointed possible roadblocks to reform within the institution, he can begin to address those challenges by soliciting the support of the institution's decisionmakers and implementers of reform. The ideal approach is two-pronged: make contact with the leadership and/or decisionmakers, and meet with the individuals who will implement new systems and practices. Capacity-building activities will depend on both of these groups of actors giving their stamp of approval to a new, more effective institutional structure or to the search for such a structure. An institution can only deliver a service (such as education or security) if it has staff members who have the capacity to perform as required. In turn, individual staff members can only use their capacity if they are within a larger institutional structure. An adviser must avoid strengthening the capacity of an individual without ensuring that the institution can capitalize on new knowledge, sharpened skills, and a changed mind-set.

The systems and mind-set of the donor community writ large are most often supply-driven. In other words, donors fund projects that serve their own interests and reflect their conception of what a competent government ministry looks like. This means that the government institutions and their staffs have little opportunity to find solutions to concrete problems; indeed, they have little opportunity even to identify the existence and nature of concrete problems.

Demand-driven approaches to strengthening capacity (i.e., approaches that give local actors and institutions what they believe will be a viable solution) are highly desirable, but they are not the norm. However, even though advisers usually have to function in supply-driven projects, they must nonetheless create demand for the transfer of knowledge. The effective adviser understands that if local actors do not perceive a problem with the existing system, they will not welcome change, and any change that is imposed will almost certainly prove temporary. In short, if change is to stick, there must be a demand for it.

In some instances, an adviser's host institution may be extremely enthusiastic about a proposed change. However, this initial enthusiasm may decrease or disappear entirely as more details emerge about the steps that need to be taken to achieve this change and as local actors realize the costs, to themselves, of changing. Costs can include loss of personal income or incentives, as well as the creation of a sense of personal insecurity because change means unacceptable losses for others. Change can impose other kinds of hardships, too, such as an increased workload, an obligation to acquire new knowledge and skills, and an end to inefficient but familiar and comfortable patterns of behavior. An institution's staff has to accept that change is difficult to accomplish, takes time, demands focused attention, and may increase workloads.

Thus, the effective adviser strives to generate buy-in for the proposed change. This can be done by identifying champions for change, by highlighting the payoffs of the proposed action, by reframing the proposal to reflect the problems as they are defined by the counterpart and/or stakeholders, and by communicating the reasons for and the consequences of the proposed change to all concerned. Seeking out people within an institution who already have formulated ideas for changing the institution is often useful; they have experienced firsthand the impacts of a weak system and they may have devised viable ways of strengthening the system. As outsiders, advisers typically find it difficult to conceive solutions that would not only remedy institutional problems, but also be accepted within the institution.

An adviser should remember that her counterpart, and even lower-level staff, may agree in principle with the need for change, but may not support it in practice because of the professional and personal costs it may entail. Change may cost the counterpart her job, for example, or, in dire cases, her life. The adviser always needs to keep in mind that she will sooner or later leave the local environment but that the counterpart will not and will have to deal with the consequences of any changes made. Acknowledging this reality will help the adviser to propose pragmatic and locally oriented solutions.

Pragmatism is also important in securing the support of the wider local community. An adviser should seek out rather than sidestep local political actors and interests, because they have the power to render any plan unworkable if they see it as a foreign imposition. Other local interest groups should also be consulted and given time to air their concerns, digest plans for reform, and contribute to those plans. Spending time explaining proposals, soliciting input, and allowing for initial reluctance to give way to acceptance is not wasting time. The more that local considerations are incorporated into the reform process, the more sustainable the new system will be.

Establishing Authority, Credibility, and Legitimacy

In most cases, the adviser will enter a mission environment in which local actors have already encountered several other individuals and organizations intent on building capacity. Unfortunately, in the past the level of preparation for a capacity-building mission, including advising missions, has often been low, resulting in a trail of mistakes and broken promises. Local actors have become skeptical about, critical of, or hostile to interveners of all kinds. Most advisers, through no fault of their own, will therefore encounter resistance from local actors.

Until recently, many advisers sought to win the respect of, or at least access to, local officials by promising donations of equipment, offering monetary rewards, and emphasizing the international power and prestige of the country or the multinational coalition spearheading the intervention. But donations and rewards did not always materialize, and even when they did, they failed to enhance the capacity of individuals and institutions.

Today, advisers have to establish a significant level of "authority" (as defined below), credibility, and legitimacy in order to secure access to local officials and stakeholders and to win their respect. Establishing and maintaining authority, credibility, and legitimacy is no easy task, but it can be done if one is mindful of the following guidelines.

Authority

In the past, under pressure from their deploying organizations to secure a particular result, advisers often sought to dictate, directly or indirectly, decisionmaking process outcomes. An effective advising mission, however, is one in which alternative approaches to problem solving and system reform are presented to a counterpart by an adviser who recognizes that the counterpart has the authority to accept or reject different approaches.

The term *authority* has several meanings, two of which are important for an adviser to keep in mind. The most common understanding of "authority" is the power to make decisions and enforce them. But *authority* can also denote the expertise that a professional possesses—and that expertise can be a rich resource for officials seeking to enhance their performance.

The effective adviser acknowledges his lack of formal authority and builds authority by demonstrating the practical value of his expertise, customizing knowledge and "denationalizing" terminology to fit the local institutional and cultural context. In other words, the effective adviser bases his authority on his credibility.

Credibility

Credibility—that is, the recognition by those who work with the adviser that the adviser knows what he is talking about and has a strong problem-solving track record—is crucial to the development of a peer-to-peer relationship between the counterpart and the adviser. The adviser must be seen as a consummate professional, with the knowledge, skills, and intelligence to devise practicable solutions to local problems. It is not sufficient for the adviser to possess those attributes; the adviser must demonstrate their value in the local context.

Personal factors can make it harder for an adviser to be seen as credible. For instance, a young adviser is likely to be regarded skeptically at first, especially if he has never been in a conflict zone before or experienced or witnessed the trauma of war. Equally, a seasoned professional who has spent twenty years managing procurement processes at home is likely, when first deployed as an adviser, to be seen by locals as irrelevant to their needs, because their system is nothing like the system in which the adviser has acquired his experience. The effective adviser recognizes that local actors will not automatically accept his expertise and professional capacities and works hard to establish that he is an expert and can be of assistance.

Credibility can be built by respecting local realities and showing the ability to customize solutions to address indigenous concerns and take into account existing levels of (and shortfalls in) competence. The adviser must recognize that some differences between his ideas and local realities are "nonnegotiable"—that is, those differences cannot be bridged, at least not in the short term. Take the example of a staff member who is illiterate but needs to read to contribute to the new system being introduced, and whose bosses want to keep him on staff because he is a member of a politically powerful clan. The adviser should not ignore the bosses' understandable concerns and insist that the staff member be replaced. Or take the example of an adviser who wants to inject democratic principles into a ministry staffed with people who have spent their entire careers in a highly authoritarian system serving a dictatorial regime. The adviser should respect and acknowledge this history, rather than brusquely repudiating it. The way forward is to gradually build a cultural bridge between the authoritarian past and a future in which people gain decisionmaking power not because of the whims of a tyrant but according to established policies, procedures, and practices.

An adviser should be willing and able to support problem solving within a highly flawed system. Gaps in capacity may be numerous, resources may be severely limited, politics may color all decisions. Respect of these realities by the advisers enhances his credibility—locals recognize that the adviser is a pragmatist, not a perfectionist; a realist, not an idealist; a colleague, not a critic.

Credibility also rests on the ability of the adviser to offer advice that addresses key issues as they are defined by the counterpart, proposing adjustments or alternatives to the status quo that are likely to make an institution or system more effective. Like a good consultant, an adviser must be able to listen strategically—asking probing questions to get specific answers that will lead to an enhanced, in-depth understanding of a situation—to what local actors are saying, to ask questions that yield helpful information, and to take into account the multilayered nuances that are at play at all times.

Legitimacy

Two interrelated audiences assess the adviser's legitimacy. The first audience is made up of local officials and other influential local actors; the second consists of the general public in the country to which the adviser is deployed. Of course, these two audiences overlap, in part because local officials and staff members are very likely to share the opinions of the general public to which they belong, and in part because the public is the end user of the services provided by the institution that the officials run. Advisers thus should see themselves as accountable to both audiences and should seek to bolster their legitimacy in the eyes of both.

The legitimacy of the adviser is tied to several factors: the perceived legitimacy of the intervention as a whole; the local reputation of the government and/or specific government agency deploying the adviser; and the adviser's conduct in the field.

In some cases—Iraq, for instance—the lack of perceived legitimacy of the entire intervention can challenge the legitimacy of a specific capacity-strengthening project. In other cases, a succession of ill-equipped, ill-trained, and/or ill-informed advisers deployed as part of the mission can shake the confidence of local actors in the ability of advisers to facilitate reform.

The identity of the adviser (e.g., the adviser's nationality, gender, age) and the reputation of the government and government agency deploying the adviser (e.g., the US Department of Justice, the Italian Caribinieri, the New Zealand Ministry of Defense) also influence the ability of the adviser to gain access and be perceived as a resource by the counterpart. Indeed, an adviser who can establish herself as a legitimate member of a legitimate mission, as it is seen by local actors, will encourage local actors to be more open to new ideas and more willing to consider advice on its merits rather than reject it out of hand.

Humility is crucial to the legitimacy-seeking efforts of advisers. An acknowledgment of the mistakes made in the past by both individual advisers and the overall intervention mission will help to persuade local actors that this adviser has learned some lessons, knows the history of the process being reformed, and is willing to play a supportive role rather than insisting on dictating solutions. In addition, respect for what has been tried before and what is part of the system in the present is important. Exhibiting this respect by asking questions and acknowledging the contributions that the past has made to present systems helps dispel suspicions that the adviser is merely the agent of a country looking to further its own national interest.

Advisers have to undertake the very delicate task of positioning themselves vis-à-vis the international community, the intervening force, and the government and agency that has deployed them. It is important to distinguish between the larger mission, which may use force and other tools that are unpopular with local actors, and the adviser's project, which joins the adviser and the counterpart. This conversation should revolve around the sharing of knowledge and practices that will enhance the ability of the individual or the institution to deliver a service to the population.

*   *   *

Fundamentally, in establishing authority, credibility, and legitimacy, the effective adviser positions herself as a *resource*. Rather than becoming part of the staff of the counterpart and the institution, the adviser serves much as a consultant does, becoming intimately familiar with the challenges the institution faces but not becoming part of the institution itself.

The effective adviser offers her expertise as a resource to solve problems that counterparts wish to address by offering ideas that emanate from the adviser's experience with similar problems back at home. However, advisers need to take great care in the way in which they cast themselves as a resource in their host environment. Advisers can make the mistake of listing their job titles, qualifications, and other credentials to counterparts, even though those credentials mean nothing in the host country. Instead, the effective adviser offers information about the common problems she may have faced at home and discusses how they were addressed. This approach allows counterparts to get a glimpse of what contributions they may expect from the adviser, which in turn is likely to encourage the counterparts to seek out the advice of the outsider.

Note

1. Helene Cooper and Thom Shanker, "U.S. Redefines Afghan Success Before Conference," *New York Times,* May 17, 2012.

5

Assessing Local Capacity

AN ADVISER'S FIRST TASK AFTER BEING DEPLOYED IS TO GET A
comprehensive understanding of the capacity that already exists in
the local environment. In the past, advisers have undervalued or
entirely ignored local capacity. Like interveners in general, advisers
have tended to assume that everything done by the host country is
done better in the advisers' own countries. This mind-set may be natural but it is problematic, and it arises from a failure to recognize that
systems, institutions, and the people involved in them are highly
dependent on their environment. Local cultures and languages have a
great impact on how local institutions evolve, as do the extent and
quality of the educational system, the size of the tax base (and hence
the size of the government's budget), the nature of the political system, prevailing political dynamics, and the country's history. Moreover, while some local institutions may be entirely ineffective in providing a public service, most have evolved not only in response to
local conditions but also to perform in local conditions. They may
not be perfect, but they are far from worthless.

As this chapter explains, an adviser who approaches her mission aware that the international community has neither all the
answers nor all the capacity is more likely to make a success of that
mission. The chapter begins by explaining the importance of the
adviser understanding the dynamics and realities on the ground and
the impact of her intervention on the situation. The chapter then

discusses the value of working with counterparts to identify not only existing capacity but also the best ways of enhancing it. The chapter concludes by describing how an effective adviser learns about existing capacity through open-ended, information-seeking questions.

Understanding the Environment and How It Is Affected by Outside Intervention

Understanding the transitioning environment in which the adviser operates is crucial to the formulation of sound advice. In the case of societies emerging from conflict, the adviser should seek to understand the interests of the various parties to the conflict, the issues at stake, the history of the conflict, and its impact on the functioning of government institutions. Unfortunately, many capacity-strengthening projects have exhibited conflict or situation blindness and have furnished aid or funded programs that have not matched local needs. The record of past interventions reveals a frequent lack of investment in coherent, integrated, and comprehensive contextual analyses, leading to unrealistic, ineffective, or counterproductive donor project design. The tendency of many donors is to shield activities from a hostile environment when instead the conflict situation should be *guiding* the project design. This means that advising activities must incorporate the messy nature and broad scope of the entire project cycle: planning, implementation, and evaluation.

It is seldom enough, however, for advisers merely to comprehend overarching conflict dynamics. In addition to undertaking *conflict analysis* (understanding the why, who, what, and when of a conflict), the effective adviser is also *conflict sensitive*. As noted in Chapter 2, conflict sensitivity involves being sensitive to the potential consequences of any kind of intervention (from a full-scale military mission to a small project shepherded by an individual adviser) on a community, its institutions, and the complex web of systems and relationships among various institutions and individuals in a country experiencing or emerging from conflict. An adviser should be aware that even his mere presence is affecting the dynamics of the local environment. An intervention in a country that is not emerging from conflict but is nonetheless undergoing a major transition has just the same potential to affect the local environment. An intervention that is sensitive to its impact on the conflict or the transition will be better able to manage potential flashpoints and less likely to inadvertently provoke crises. Figure 5.1 shows the dynamic relationships between the key stakeholders in any transitioning context, the issues at stake, the local environment, and the adviser's activities.

The kind of unhelpful impact that an adviser can have can be illustrated by reference to the common problem of "ghost payrolls." There are two common types of ghost payrolls: one involves paying people who are indeed on the payroll but who do not actually show up for work; the other involves corrupt officials inflating the number of staff who are supposed to be working for an institution and then siphoning off the money that is set aside to pay those (nonexistent) staff. The introduction of an outside expert, the adviser, will inevitably lead to a discussion of the institution's personnel and payroll. While local officials know the crippling effect of ghost payrolls on the institution's budget, they also know the many consequences that addressing that problem may cause (e.g., angering or alienating those individuals—and the clans, sects, or ethnic groups of which they are members—who depend on their "ghostly" income to support their families). These consequences may seem to the officials to outweigh the potential benefits of reducing the ghost payroll. As a result, local actors, although they know the problem exists, may have chosen to do nothing about it. But an adviser who is determined to

Figure 5.1 The Adviser's Impact on the Environment

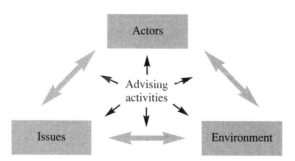

tackle the phantom payroll may offer suggestions for doing so, putting the officials in the uncomfortable position of either rejecting his advice and appearing to condone corruption or taking steps to reduce the ghost payroll and in the process angering colleagues and powerful local actors who have been benefiting from the fraud. Even if the counterpart wants to tackle the problem, doing so while the adviser is in the institution may make the counterpart look as though he is doing the bidding of the intervening powers.

Assume That There Is Local Capacity and Look for It

All capacity-building missions must assume that local capacity exists, leverage it, and strengthen what works rather than ignore it and build next to it. In all countries, even brand-new ones, systems (for managing staff, administrating benefits, managing logistics, maintaining equipment, and so forth) are in place, and there are always individuals who have ideas for enhancing practices, procedures, and competences. To get a comprehensive picture of what capacity exists, the adviser must talk not only with her counterpart but also with many different kinds of stakeholders.

Strategic listening is the key to the adequate diagnosis of a problem, as it is only by asking questions about how things are done that the causes of ineffective practices can be identified. By identifying the knowledge base that is already integrated into the system, the adviser will then be able to design an approach that capitalizes on that base instead of seeking to build a new system from scratch.

In order to diagnose problems and propose ideas and approaches, one must first demonstrate respect, which includes showing interest in the capacity that locals already possess. Like any expert (e.g., a therapist, an attorney, a doctor), the adviser should try to devise a solution that draws on existing knowledge and can make use of existing structures.

As discussed in Chapter 4, ignoring what already exists, even if it is weak, is insulting to local counterparts and counterproductive to the strengthening of capacity. Take the example of a public works minister who is waiting for a team of Western advisers who are tasked with assisting the minister in strengthening the ability of her ministry to provide public utilities. The team of advisers arrives in her office bearing many engineering plans and proposals. This is the team's first meeting with the minister. After exchanging pleasantries, the team proceeds to present a water-purification system that it wants to implement on behalf of the minister. The minister, however, tells the team that her country has been purifying water for a very long time and that she will not require the team's services. In this case, the advisers had neglected to learn about the existing capacities of the public works ministry and wrongly assumed that the country was not able to provide clean water to any of the population. The advisers not only were uninformed but also failed to ask questions. Rather than beginning their advising mission with a plan and solutions, they should have formulated questions that would have allowed them to understand the reasons for the current gaps in capacity. For instance, the ministry might be able to purify water, but it may not be able to secure the water-delivery infrastructure against damage, readily procure the products required to clean water, or routinely maintain purification equipment.

Co-analysis of Desired Outcome

Co-analysis of desired outcome is a tool to help an adviser guide the assessment of existing capacity and interpret the information gathered. Co-analysis rests on two premises. One is that counterparts and local stakeholders are better positioned than the adviser is to judge the viability of reform efforts and thus should participate in analyzing what capacity already exists and, by implication, what additional capacity is required. The second premise is that local actors, while they need assistance, have a significant amount of capacity that can be used as a foundation of the knowledge transfer project. This process of co-analysis must be customized to fit the local context. No two situations are exactly alike, of course, and no two analyses of those situations should be identical in approach, content, and implications.

With this caveat about customization in mind, advisers can use a three-step process to help structure their co-analysis (Figure 5.2). The process assumes a continuous discussion between the adviser and the counterpart, with the adviser gradually offering ideas and alternative approaches as the consultations progress.

Figure 5.2 A Three-Step Process for Co-analysis of Desired Outcome

Existing capacity
+
Additional knowledge needed

=

Desired ability to function/
perform tasks effectively

Step 1: *Identify and establish existing capacity with counterpart.*

Ask probing questions of the counterpart and other relevant actors to identify necessary knowledge and skills and produce an assessment of existing capacity. For example, "How do you organize the trash pickup routes in your city?"

The goal of this phase is to identify the following:

Who does what?

Using what means?

What do they understand about the necessary processes/ practices?

How sophisticated is their approach?

Step 2: *Identify the tasks that allow for the effective functioning of a process or system.*

Step 3: *Identify the specific knowledge and skills necessary for the counterpart to perform his function so that the process or system will function properly.*

Asking Questions to Assess Capacity

To assess the existing capacity of relevant actors and systems, an adviser must ask many questions. Asking questions, however, can be challenging for at least three reasons. First, as experienced professionals, advisers are more accustomed to answering questions than to asking them. Second, Western professionals tend to quickly glaze over problems and move swiftly to identifying solutions. Third, in some cases, advisers believe that they understand the problem before them because they subconsciously think that all problems are similar to problems they have seen before—and thus questions are superfluous. But the effective adviser will recognize and seek to repress these tendencies, and will spend a significant amount of time asking probing questions. Indeed, at the beginning of a mission, most of an adviser's sentences should end in a question mark. A questioning approach—as opposed to say a didactic approach—will help the adviser earn a reputation for humility, respect, and empathy while identifying local ideas for sustainable solutions. Furthermore, formulating appropriate, astute, and well-informed questions will significantly enhance the standing of the adviser as a credible authority in her area of expertise and as someone who has a legitimate place in the quest to reform systems, practices, and procedures.

Asking questions can help build rapport (as discussed in the next chapter) and demonstrate respect—but only if the questions have a specific purpose, facilitate the collaborative sharing of information, and demonstrate a sensitivity to the local context. Capacity-strengthening efforts are undertaken only because of a recognized lack of capacity within institutions and/or among members of those institutions. The effective adviser takes great care not to let that unspoken but well understood reality come through in her interactions with counterparts. Some questions facilitate dialogue and foster a constructive professional relationship, but others suggest disrespect and a lack of understanding of or interest in the nuances of the environment. As a general rule, it is best to formulate questions that start with the words "What" or "How" rather than "Who," "Why," or even "Where." "What" and "How" questions suggest an interest in learning about processes and practices, challenges and opportunities. For instance: "What are the steps of the process that inventory the equipment that your troops use on a daily basis?" "How do soldiers know which equipment to take on duty with them?" "Who," "Where," and "Why" questions ask for analysis, can convey an opinion or concern, and may even look to assign blame; they can imply that there was a better way to proceed all along, making the recipient of the question uncomfortable. For instance: "Why do you have your soldiers drop off their equipment in this area?" "Who is responsible for ensuring the equipment is maintained?" In most instances, counterparts will be much more open to answering the first set of questions than the second. The second may have implications that counterparts may not wish to explore, and hence they will not foster discussion or an adviser's in-depth understanding of the situation.

Assessment answers can come in two forms: those that yield data and those that prompt analysis. Data is the more desirable type of information in an assessment, because it forms the basis for the adviser's own analysis of processes, dynamics, and realities that reveal areas of existing capacity, areas where capacity is insufficient, and faults in structures and/or systems. An interviewee's analysis has a more limited value to assessments, because it reflects his opinion of the outcome of a system or service. This information is valuable for an impact evaluation of a program or a project, but it offers little insight into the viability and effectiveness of services, systems, and structures.

The feature box below contains five broad categories of questions that can help guide the development of a useful and sensitive assessment. In each case, they must be customized to fit the local context and each interviewee. They form a framework for a flexible questionnaire that the adviser should draft prior to meeting his counterpart—and that the adviser should depart from if a conversation moves into unexpected, potentially interesting avenues. The adviser should not require the counterpart to undergo a rigid interview process. An inflexible approach will make the counterpart feel that he is being evaluated and judged, and the counterpart will respond with cautious answers that offer limited information.

While the questionnaire should be adhered to, it should nonetheless be treated as a useful reminder of the main points to be covered. Getting off track while listening to a counterpart is easy, especially in a foreign environment. Though the information that the counterpart is presenting might be interesting, it may be difficult to see its applicability in the local context. In some cultures, information is conveyed through storytelling, and advisers can gain valuable insights by listening to such stories. An adviser should listen strategically, not only hearing what the counterpart is eager to impart, but also making sure that the interviewee provides the information that the adviser needs to know. This can be a challenging task for an adviser who is struggling to navigate foreign organizational and social-cultural environments; many advisers have reported being crippled by the fear of committing cultural gaffes and have consequently followed the counterpart's conversational lead at all times. Unfortunately, information gleaned by such excessive politeness is not always useful to the advising effort. A conversation is most productive when it remains on track, with the goal of understanding the good, the bad, and the ugly of a system.

Guiding Questions for Assessing Existing Capacity

1. *What capacity currently exists?*
What expertise is available?
What are the budgets and finances?
What are the relevant networks?
Wherein does trust lie? And mistrust?
What practices are in place?
What needs are being met?
Who are the movers and the shakers?
What are the institutional frameworks? How do they function?

2. *What capacity is required?*
What knowledge is needed for a task to be consistently and effectively performed?
What skills are needed?

3. *What are the shortfalls of the existing capacity?*
How are official actors not equipped to make informed decisions?
What knowledge and skills are not integrated in existing systems, procedures, and/or practices that would be required for consistent and effective delivery of services?

(continues)

4. *What are the gaps in capacity that can be filled?*
What systems are in place?
What services are delivered as a result?

5. *What has been tried in the past?*
Who tried it?
With what resources?
With what partners?
What were the impacts?
Who benefited from it? Who suffered from it?

6

Identifying All
the Agents of Change

HAVING ASSESSED LOCAL CAPACITY, THE ADVISER'S NEXT TASK IS
to locate the individuals who either need to change in order for
capacity to be strengthened ("targets of change") or who can help the
adviser introduce the required change ("change agents"). This chapter explains how to identify both types. First, however, the chapter
discusses the importance of locating "willing partners for change"—
individuals who support change and can provide the adviser with
valuable information and ideas.

The adviser must identify not only the challenges that will stand
in the way of change but also the various mechanisms and catalysts
of change, as well as interests and goals of the various local actors
who will have to be part of any transition. The adviser's very existence in an environment means change is of the essence, a change
that has to be effectively managed from the very beginning by
involving local actors as soon as possible and as often as possible in
the reform process.

Identifying Willing Partners for Change

When the adviser arrives in country, she will quickly discover that
some local actors are willing to support the adviser's mission
whereas others are determined to resist it. Everyone has their own

reasons for being cooperative or not. The uncooperative, for example, may have had unhappy experiences with advisers in the past, or they may believe that outsiders cannot provide the assistance needed, or they may regard foreign assistance as a matter of providing funding rather than advice.

Fortunately, in any environment there are always people who support the idea of change and have strong ideas about why or how it should take place. The human resources manager who administers the payroll for police officers may be annoyed that there are fewer officers at roll call than on the payroll documents. The contracting officer may be fed up finding an empty office every time he tries to get a contract signed. The logistics manager may be exasperated by the fact that the amount of ammunition put on a truck at the depot is usually more than the amount that reaches the barracks. These individuals are part of the system and know its weaknesses all too well. They may also have excellent ideas about how to tweak a system to fix or at least reduce the impact of those weaknesses. These are the people that the adviser needs to identify and learn from.

Finding change-minded individuals, however, can be difficult. The adviser's official counterpart is unlikely to fall into this category, because high-ranking officials (as counterparts typically are) tend to benefit from the institutional status quo. In many cases, the leadership in an institution has structured procedures and practices in a manner that makes them gatekeepers of a patronage system and benefits them personally in terms of power and political and/or social status. Change therefore threatens institutional leaders with the loss of some advantage on which they have depended for many years. Moreover, in some cases a leader's personal security may be endangered by reforms that anger a beneficiary of the existing system.

Lower-ranking members of the staff are more likely to be change agents, because they have experienced firsthand the shortcomings of the present system and may have come up with ideas to address those problems. For instance, a member of staff at a police station may have witnessed the mistreatment of women who come to the station to complain of being victimized. That staff member can see that male police officers are abusing the women and that a woman police officer, if available, would provide a much more professional service to women complainants.

For the adviser, therefore, the staff rather than the leadership is a good place to look for people who have ideas for practicable and sustainable change. Engaging lower-ranking staff, it should be emphasized, can be very challenging, especially in an environment that places great value on hierarchical relationships and formality. Lower-level staff members may be reticent to discuss the inner workings of the system and any shortcomings of the officials for whom they work, even if they are well aware of such problems. Nonetheless, the insights and ideas of the staff can be gleaned by an adviser who is attentive in meetings to implicit as well as explicit critiques of existing procedures and policies. The adviser also can signal that she is looking for ideas that are homegrown and that will work in the local context. In addition, a comprehensive assessment of existing capacity, involving discussions with staff members as well as counterparts, will almost always reveal untapped capacities and ideas for alternative approaches. It is very important for the adviser to ask what has been tried before and what has not, and to seek to understand why. Homegrown ideas have the added benefit of being more acceptable to staff and leadership than proposals from foreign actors.

In short, change-minded staff members are a source of invaluable ideas and information. Their ideas for how to reform the institutions for which they work may be incorporated into and/or inspire the adviser's own plans for reform—indeed, their ideas are likely to be better-informed than the adviser's and thus more practicable. And the information that change-minded staff members possess can help the adviser determine who belongs in the "targets of change" category and who belongs in the "change agents" category.

Targets of Change

Targets of change are those individuals whose behavior must change in order for an institution—and consequently its delivery of public services—to become more effective. In the case of a ministry of interior, the targets of change are likely to be the police and those who staff the police force's support mechanisms. In the case of a ministry of health, the targets of change are service providers such as nurses, doctors, and clinic administrators, as well as all their support systems, such as the systems for procuring and transporting medical supplies, managing human resources, and setting and monitoring standards for medical practitioners.

Targets of change fall into two broad categories. The first category consists of the people whose behavior needs to change when they directly experience a problem or are at risk of experiencing it. These targets of change have to share in the responsibility of making a system work. For example, parents have to take their children to be vaccinated to send them to school; victims of crime have to report crimes and serve as witnesses in criminal trials.

The second category comprises people who contribute to the problem through their action or inaction. Strengthening capacity involves changing the behavior of these people. To qualify as targets of change, however, they must be seen by the adviser not only as contributing to a current problem but also as capable of changing their behavior so that they can contribute to a future improvement. Targets of change can be individuals who have too little capacity to perform their institutional function adequately, who behave in ways that are detrimental to the service they are meant to be delivering, or who want to alter their behavior but have too few assets and resources to do so.

Some groups can find themselves in both categories. For instance, the police may belong to the first category because they suffer from a lack of security, but if they are corrupt or poorly trained, they may also belong to the second category because they are unable to contribute to an improvement in security.

An awareness of such overlaps (between groups that are at risk and need change and those who can make the change occur but lack the capacity to do so) will help the adviser factor all relevant actors, issues, and interactions into the planning process and identify promising alternative approaches to current practices. A comprehensive understanding of environmental factors will also enhance the implementation of new approaches.

When it comes to identifying targets of change, the adviser should ask the following questions:

- What is the problem?
- Who is affected by the problem?
- Who has been affected previously by the problem?
- Who is at risk of being affected?

- Who is causing the problem? Are those responsible solely within the institution, or are secondary actors also involved?
- By what actions or inactions are they causing the problem?
- Whose behavior has recently changed but still needs support?

As explained in Chapter 4, the adviser should formulate questions that ask for data from the respondent rather than for analysis. Most people when prompted with a question will likely provide their own analysis of the situation. But the adviser has very limited information about and understanding of the framework of analysis of the respondent. Data are thus far more valuable, giving the adviser the information with which to build his own analysis of the situation and to identify problems and solutions. Analysis will be volunteered but questions should focus on data collection.

Change Agents

A "change" agent carries that label because he has the authority to change course. Political considerations are often key factors in the decision to allow and enable change. Individuals who are in positions of power over the functioning of an entire government institution or one of its departments can promote and implement reforms that will enhance the institution's systems. However, having authority to effect change is not enough. Individuals may be in the position to alter the systems in their institutions but decline to do so for a variety of reasons: a lack of political and/or institutional buy-in; a belief that the existing system is "good enough" albeit not ideal; a poorly trained staff and no opportunity to retrain it; a reluctance to lose the personal, political, or professional benefits that the current system confers. A change agent is thus a person who not only has authority and political capital but also is open to using it and knows which approaches will be viable and sustainable politically, financially, and structurally.

Change agents can influence decisions and alter behavior in two ways. First, they have the authority to order a change in a system or approach. Second, they can work with the individuals who suffer from the lack of capacity of a system, raising their awareness of the negative consequences of a specific behavior, lack of competence, or weaknesses of a system.

A credible and trustworthy change agent who is concerned for the welfare of the population can be an invaluable partner for the adviser. Among other assets, such a partner brings to the project firsthand understanding of the nature of the problem being tackled, an awareness of the nuances and sensitivities of the local environment that may go undetected by the adviser, and the ability to diagnose shortcomings and propose remedies in a way that local officials are likely to accept.

An adviser looking for a change agent to partner with should ask the following kinds of questions:

- Who has the power to bring about change?
- Wherein lies the will for change? Wherein lies the capacity for change?
- Who has the desire, time, resources, and incentive to bring about change?
- Who currently lacks that desire but might be persuaded to champion or embrace change?
- Who has relationships with the people whose support is necessary for change to occur?
- Who do the targets of change trust?
- To whom do the targets of change listen?

The Dynamics of Change: An Example

Change occurs when both agents and targets of change are engaged.

Take the scenario in which, when police equipment is moved by trucks from the depot to the barracks, some of that equipment is missing when the trucks reach their destination. The loss may be the result of ineffective management of the shipment, or of part of the shipment being "paid" to bandits for safe passage along roads they control, or of the driver selling some of the equipment en route. Whatever the reason, the ineffective shipment of equipment can translate into the loss of life of underequipped police officers and/or their impaired ability to prevent crime and enforce the laws.

(continues)

The "necessary change" in this scenario is for entire shipments to arrive at their destination consistently.

The targets of change, those whose behavior has to change in order to improve the system, include everyone who is part of the process of shipping the equipment, from those in charge of its procurement to those who draw up bills of lading of the equipment and those who drive the trucks. It is easy to see how these individuals can contribute to the system productively or destructively.

The change agents include those whose decisions will structure the procurement and logistics aspects of the shipping of the police equipment. They have to introduce a system of punishments (and perhaps also rewards) to ensure that each of the different links in the chain of procurement of police perform their tasks appropriately. These change agents include procurement managers and their staffs, logistics management directors and their staff, and security providers for dangerous routes.

7

How to Transfer Knowledge

HAVING IDENTIFIED HER TARGET AUDIENCES, THE ADVISER CAN now press ahead with the single most important aspect of the mission: transferring knowledge. Obviously, this is a task that requires the adviser to have considerable technical expertise in the relevant subject matter (e.g., logistics or human resources); the adviser has to possess knowledge in order to be able to transfer it. But the task of transferring knowledge also requires some expertise in knowledge transfer itself; the adviser has to know how to transfer the knowledge she possesses.

This chapter helps advisers who are expert in their own fields, but not so expert in the art of communicating that expertise, by laying out general guidelines for transferring knowledge. It begins by emphasizing the importance of dialogue—of conversations not only between the adviser and her counterpart but also between counterparts and stakeholders. As the opening section explains, to make such conversations productive, the adviser needs to become a "facilitator." The next—and longest—section of the chapter offers an introduction to the methods and principles of adult learning. Adults learn in a different way than do teenagers and children, and the adviser needs to recognize this and to take advantage of the approaches that have been shown to work best with older students. The third and final section points out that many of those learners will have experienced some trauma during the armed conflict or political upheaval that their society has recently undergone. The adviser, who needs to be sensitive to this trauma, may find Maslow's hierarchy of needs useful. A combination of conflict sensitivity and learning-style savvy can go a long way toward making an adviser's tour more productive.

Facilitating Conversation

An effective adviser is a "facilitator." A facilitator is someone who helps a group of people understand their common objectives and assists them in planning to achieve those goals, but who does not take a particular position in the discussion. Advisers act as facilitators when they introduce ideas for channeling available resources, promote brainstorming about how to circumvent obstacles, and encourage the evaluation of possible strategies.

Facilitation is attractive for an adviser in part because she lacks the official authority to make and implement decisions and thus must seek to influence the decisionmaking process of others. However, facilitation is by no means a poor substitute for executive control. To the contrary, facilitation helps to unlock or nurture several of the most valuable resources for any knowledge transfer effort: local ideas, local support, and local ownership.

Facilitation has three main goals within the context of a knowledge transfer mission. First, it encourages the full participation of all concerned parties so that their resulting reflection—the process of weighing of the pros and cons of ideas of various parties and the identification of necessary resources and conditions—can be discussed and understood by all stakeholders.

Second, a facilitated discussion promotes mutual understanding. Facilitation allows the adviser to invite counterparts and relevant staff and stakeholders to address their challenges and limitations, to recognize the opportunities they already have, to identify the opportunities they are seeking, and to determine what resources they need and what resources are available. Facilitation promotes the validation of gaps in capacity by giving counterparts the opportunity to identify, describe, and discuss gaps; as they do this, counterparts buy into the need to seek a solution to the problem. The validation of others promotes a collaborative mind-set. Indeed, as the participants most affected by a particular issue testify to its impact on them, other participants begin to empathize, setting in motion a process that allows them to make compromises that they may not otherwise make.

Third, facilitation cultivates shared responsibility. The practice of strengthening capacity through the transfer of knowledge requires that the individuals targeted for change accept the need to change how they operate and to alter their mind-sets. Without this buy-in, the solution implemented likely will be unsustainable. Facilitation allows responsibility to be allocated on a voluntary basis. An adviser can promote the willingness of participants to take on some portion of the burden that reform forces on stakeholders, eliciting buy-in from the "operators" of the newly reformed systems.

To be a good facilitator, one must be a good listener, an active listener. As explained in Chapter 3, an active listener listens to what their interlocutors say for information that helps the listener build a comprehensive understanding of an issue or situation. An active listener also asks follow-up questions to maximize her understanding of the relevant issues, facts, and factors that point to a gap in capacity or, alternatively, a potential resource. A simple guideline for those who want to become good listeners is to begin asking questions in a tone that connotes interest in, and even a sense of respect for, the perceptions and actions of local actors.

Other, more general guidelines to keep in mind for a successful facilitation process include the following:

- Lead but do not dominate discussion; suggest a direction in which the discussion can proceed.
- Be prepared to ask specific, targeted, probing questions to help participants identify their own, as well as other participants', perspectives and opinions.
- Be knowledgeable enough to be able to ask guiding questions.
- Help participants find connections between their ideas and opinions.
- Avoid providing an answer: guide the group on a journey to a place where they can find the answers themselves.
- Be patient enough to allow participants to arrive at those answers.
- Affirm and recognize good ideas.
- Allow silence; participants may be thinking a great deal even if they are not speaking a lot.

- Promote the concept of a "safe space" in which participants can speak frankly without fear of suffering repercussions (such as losing their position, power, status, relationships, or resources) or being held accountable for whatever changes are eventually made.
- Allow participants to use their imagination to brainstorm, but bring the conversation back to ground when ideas become too abstract.
- Challenge participants to think differently than usual and identify alternatives.

Adult Learning Principles in an Advising Context

Change almost always requires a learning process. Local officials and other actors need to learn new knowledge, skills, and approaches if they are to devise and implement solutions to the obstacles impeding the performance of local institutions. Part of the job of the adviser is to teach counterparts what they need to know.

In some cases, local actors can help the adviser identity what knowledge and skills are required. Advisers may enjoy sharing information that they possess that the local officials want to learn. In many cases, however, the adviser faces the task of introducing information that local stakeholders have *not* identified as significant. As early as the assessment phase, the adviser who asks the right questions will likely identify gaps in capacity that are not well understood or defined by local actors. Teaching people what they don't know they need to know can be a difficult and uncomfortable experience. The task can be even more challenging because "students" in postconflict environments are likely to have experienced significant trauma, which should be accounted for in the methodology of their teachers.

In order to transfer the knowledge deemed likely to be useful to the counterpart, the adviser needs to have a good understanding of how adults learn new skills and acquire new knowledge. The teaching of adults is called "andragogy," and it is based on a substantial body of research that shows that adults learn in different ways than children do. The role of the teacher of an adult is that of helper, guide, encourager, consultant, and resource rather than that of transmitter, disciplinarian, judge, or authority.

The education and training-related needs of an individual changes once a person reaches adulthood. Many of the skills that the person acquired as a young student will have become outmoded, and he needs to be persuaded to engage in lifelong learning in order to remain a useful member of staff throughout his career. An effective training program is one that infuses participants with heightened curiosity and an increased ability to carry on their own learning once the program ends. The teacher should strive to bring the learner along a continuum of maturity in learning from being a passive recipient of knowledge to an active inquirer who seeks knowledge. The material to be learned should respond to a yearning to enhance one's ability to perform. To stimulate such an appetite, the material that makes up the content of the teaching should be presented in a way that has real meaning to learners. Adult learners are voluntary learners and therefore demand knowledge and skills that are of practical value and will enhance their performance.

From an adviser's perspective, teaching serves institutional as well as personal needs and goals. In the first place, it provides the staff of institutions the skills and knowledge that they need to contribute to the mission of the organization. Second, it contributes to an improvement in institutional performance of the tasks that are central to the adviser's mission. And third, it can nurture public understanding, or at the very least awareness, of the capacity-strengthening efforts undertaken by the institution and its staff. Strengthening the skills and knowledge of adults maintains and promotes the progress of the wider society as well as the individuals and the institutions to which they belong.

Three Models of Adult Teaching

The transfer of knowledge in capacity-strengthening projects can be accomplished in various ways. In his 1995 study of how to teach conflict resolution skills to adults, John Paul Lederach outlined three distinct models that can be employed: prescriptive, adaptive, and elicitive.

The *prescriptive* method is typically used when specific skills, usually technical skills, are needed to raise capacity levels and when the adviser has determined that a viable solution to the capacity gap does not exist locally. According to this method, the adviser identifies specific topics to teach that will address the problem as she sees it.

The *adaptive* method is appropriate when there is no single right answer and when knowledge-transfer tasks involve helping counterparts and stakeholders to identify the most effective and efficient options. This approach gives the adviser the opportunity to share ideas with the counterpart and to encourage the counterpart to adapt or customize one or more of those ideas to the local context, taking into consideration the existing challenges and opportunities. The adviser then needs to teach decisionmaking skills, including the need to take account of all relevant factors.

The *elicitive* approach involves the most participation from the counterpart. This method is best suited for high-ranking officials or highly experienced technical staff who have the ability to assess information, ideas, and opinions, and to share them with the adviser. They must also possess significant motivation to usher in change by enhancing individual and institutional capacity. The adviser's role is focused on facilitating the formulation of ideas and vetting those ideas for their applicability and viability. The elicitive method usually generates more learning than the prescriptive and adaptive approaches, because the counterpart's own process of reflection teaches him as much as what the adviser has to share. The counterpart has knowledge but does not necessarily have the opportunity to reflect and arrange his thoughts; the elicitive approach provides that opportunity.[1]

Which of these methods is used by the adviser should vary according to the specific demands of her project. An adviser should become familiar with all models of knowledge transfer and borrow from them to customize an approach that suits the adviser's target audience. The elicitive method is likely to be the most suitable for the majority of advising missions and projects, but an adviser may well find it helpful to customize her approach by blending elements of all three methods.

Useful Principles of Adult Learning

The role of the teacher of adults is to help students discover better ways of performing a specific function and thus meet their personal or institutional goals. Effective advisers help counterparts identify their learning needs and develop a plan for how to obtain the necessary knowledge and skills. This is not an intuitive task for most advisers, because adult education is rarely their career, although it may be part of their job description if they are supervisors, administrators, managers, or group leaders. An adviser, however, can become a significantly better teacher if she incorporates into her work some of the key principles of andragogy. This section presents nine of these principles:

- Identify gaps in knowledge and skills.
- Create an environment for brainstorming.
- Offer a logical sequence and reinforce key information.
- Give control over what to learn to the learner.
- Share information that can be useful immediately.
- Establish a respectful relationship with the learner.
- Make clear that the adviser is a partner, not a professor.
- Be part of the team.
- Be accountable.[2]

Identify Gaps in Knowledge and Skills

As discussed earlier, the effective adviser assumes that some level of adequate capacity exists locally and identifies the knowledge and the skills, as well as the relevant procedures and practices, that make up that capacity. Once the adviser and the counterpart have mapped out the existing capacity and the gaps within it, they can draw up a list of skills, knowledge, and attributes that are missing and develop a plan for acquiring them.

A needs assessment must be conducted in order to reveal to the adviser, the counterpart, and anyone else who should be part of the change process the areas in which the existing system needs to be improved. A needs assessment will ultimately shape the content of the curriculum by spotlighting what the learners—counterparts and staff—need to learn. Without an understanding of what gaps in knowledge and skills exist, the adviser may well make the mistake of importing a ready-made procedure from another institution or country. A ready-made "solution" may be easier and quicker to implement, but it is very likely to be only part of the solution, or even counterproductive, because it temporarily shores up a system that cannot be sustained over the long term.

If the human resources staff in a ministry needs to learn how to incorporate women as employees, the adviser should map the specific obstacles in the way of realizing that goal and then share that map with the counterpart, who can decide how to overcome or circumvent those obstacles. A needs assessment may reveal that although ministry officials believe that women perform tasks well and would be useful additions to the ministry's staff, the ministry has no procedure for recruiting women. Establishing a procedure to recruit women will require an understanding of the training and education needs of the staff for them to maintain a recruitment program long after the adviser has left the country.

Create an Environment for Brainstorming

This principle stresses the importance of not exposing the mistakes that the learner makes. As a counterpart listens to an idea that the adviser shares, the counterpart must feel comfortable asking questions, however basic or even unrelated they may be. The counterpart (and staff) will refrain from further interaction with the adviser if he is made to feel like an ignorant student. The process of sharing expertise must be one in which all parties involved feel that they are valued participants in a process of building knowledge and developing solutions.

For an adult, learning can be an uncomfortable experience and the idea of having to learn can be hard to accept. In postconflict or transitioning environments, adults often face the daunting task of having to learn how to function in an environment that is foreign to them. They also have to adapt to a new normal. The effective adviser recognizes the discomfort that counterparts and other actors may feel when they have to learn changed behavior or adopt a new mind-set. For example, a police officer may find it difficult to respect the rights of alleged perpetrators when that officer has spent many years working for a system that routinely disrespected rights. The police officer may feel that he has been arresting individuals wrongly for many years, which is not a productive thought for someone who is being asked to open his mind to new approaches and practices.

Adult learners only integrate new knowledge, skills, and perspectives when the instructional environment allows the learners to make mistakes when practicing newly acquired skills or applying new knowledge. The effective adviser thus creates an atmosphere in which counterparts and other actors feel free to ask questions, try new practices, and share ideas with fellow professionals without fear of being shamed or having their personal and/or professional reputations tainted. The learner should be helped to realize that people learn every day and that learning does not stop when formal education ends.

Offer a Logical Sequence and Reinforce Key Information

The process of transferring knowledge must make sense to the learner. The presentation of new information must have its own logic and be accompanied by a justification for the selected content of the teaching. Moreover, knowledge should be transferred in a comprehensible sequence: adult learners need to see the beginning of the process, to follow the steps as the process unfolds, and to advance all the way to the end. And as they move forward, the pace of learning should accelerate and the content of learning should grow more challenging. In short, begin at the beginning, accelerate from slow to fast, and move from easy to hard.

Newly acquired knowledge and skills should be reinforced by giving learners an opportunity to identify the ways in which they can make use of what they have just learned. The adviser should organize role-playing exercises, facilitate debates, and otherwise help build the learners' confidence that they can put their new skills into practice.

Give Control over What to Learn to the Learner

Counterparts should feel in control of their acquisition of the skills and knowledge required to perform their functions at an enhanced capacity level. Counterparts usually regard advisers as foreign colleagues, not as teachers in the traditional sense, and expect advisers to treat them with the respect that colleagues afford one another. If a counterpart does not feel respected, she will learn much less.

As suggested in the co-analysis framework presented in Chapter 5, the counterpart and adviser should jointly establish learning objectives and then discuss how best to achieve those objectives (e.g., they might discuss the respective merits of a training program and a mentoring program). They can discuss methodology between themselves in private or with a group of staff members who have been identified as in need of new knowledge and skills. The goal should be to allow the learner—whether the counterpart or the staff members—to help determine the nature and scope of what they will learn as well as the methodology for learning it.

Information should be delivered to adult learners, especially in postconflict environments, visually as well as by the spoken word. Visual material tends to provoke a stronger emotional response and, therefore, is more likely to interest the learner looking for a solution to a frustrating or infuriating problem. Personal accounts and anecdotes that reveal shortcomings in the existing system may parallel the learner's situation, and related discussions may lead to the formulation of new ideas.

Stimulating feelings and ideas will likely affect the learner's behavior, because increased awareness often inspires a learner to change his behavior. This is another reason to employ interactive knowledge-transfer practices such as role-playing simulations. Being in the shoes of a specific actor in a realistic scenario is particularly instructive for decisionmaking learning and for fostering an understanding of other actors' options and constraints, which in turn may encourage a readiness to cooperate or compromise.

Share Information That Can Be Useful Immediately

Immediacy is very important in terms of the nature and scope of the content that the adviser shares with learners. This principle reminds us that adults, especially professionals looking to improve their performance, will learn if the material being taught is immediately useful to them. The effective adviser decides what to teach and how to teach it—including the choice of learning activities and materials—according to this principle of immediacy. If a new skill or approach is not immediately useful to the learner, and is not recognized by the learner as being useful, it is unlikely to be adopted.

The effective adviser encourages the counterpart and any other relevant actors to identify current obstacles to better performance and existing gaps in capacity in the needs assessment and co-analysis they perform when planning their project. The temptation to broker information that does not seem immediately useful to the learner should be resisted, as should the inclination to prioritize efforts to tackle problems that concern the adviser but not her counterpart. For example, a ministry suffers from endemic corruption but its most pressing problem is an ineffective procurement procedure. The effective adviser thus identifies solutions to enhance the procurement system and resists the temptation to address corruption, at least for the moment. Safeguards for corrupt practices can be incorporated later, as the procurement system is strengthened. Corruption may not be an issue that requires immediate attention for the procurement manager. Advisers have to pay special attention to making the connection between learning objectives and the knowledge and skills they attempt to teach.

Establish a Respectful Relationship with the Learner

The relationship between a person with problem-solving abilities and experience to share (the adviser) and a person who would benefit from learning some hard-learned lessons (the counterpart) should rest on mutual respect for what each brings to that relationship. Such respect can exist only if the counterpart remains independent of, rather than becoming dependent on, the assistance provided by the adviser. The preservation of mutual respect also requires that the relationship remain professional rather than personal, so as to maintain the teacher-learner distinction.

Make Clear That the Adviser Is a Partner, Not a Professor

The adviser, while in a teaching role, has to be mindful to maintain a peer-to-peer relationship with the counterpart. The adviser may wish to share insights and lessons learned with a counterpart, but if the learner sees the adviser as "the professor" with whom one cannot disagree or debate, there will be little discussion and no learning will take place. The counterpart will respond well to the intervention of the adviser only if the latter treats the counterpart as a colleague. Furthermore, both parties must be in no doubt that the authority to effect change remains with the counterpart and that the information received is a resource to be considered in decisionmaking, not a diktat.

The effective adviser articulates very simply and clearly why he is "in country." The more concretely an adviser can explain his role

to local officials and stakeholders and the more clearly they understand that the adviser is there as a peer and partner, the more persua-
sive the adviser will be in explaining how he can contribute to
resolving the problems that officials and stakeholders face.

Be Part of the Team

It is very important for the adviser to establish himself as part of a
team rather than as a teacher. The formation of a team with the
counterpart, staff members, and other relevant partners offers safety
in the learning experience. When team members feel the sense of
personal safety that comes with being part of a larger group—a
group that shares responsibility for learning how to operate and contribute to a new system or process—every team member will be
more open to taking in new information and accepting new practices. The risk of failure becomes diluted and the likelihood that one
person will be blamed explicitly for an ill-designed process is significantly lessened.

Furthermore, the sense of teamwork may carry over into the
future, as team members and their colleagues implement the new
practices. The content of any program that aims to transfer knowledge should seek to identify the concepts, attitudes, and skills necessary for successful teamwork in the counterpart's specific context.
When many actors in a system are forced to relearn various functions
and even shift mind-sets, each actor should envision their contribution as part of a much larger effort. The effective adviser encourages
this attitude by adopting a teaching methodology that involves exercises that help the institution staff identify themselves as parts of a
larger system, which in turn encourages them to coordinate and even
collaborate to resolve problems across departments.

Be Accountable

Both the learner/counterpart and the teacher/adviser should be
accountable for the success of the learning process. The counterpart
is accountable for revealing enough information to the adviser to
allow the process of assessing gaps and devising solutions to move
forward. In addition, given that it is extremely difficult to force
someone to learn something that they do not wish to learn, a counter-

part who agrees to give and receive information and begin to develop a project with the adviser is accountable to himself for learning what the project requires the counterpart to learn.

On the other side of the learner-teacher relationship, the adviser is expected to share adequate information with the counterpart. The adviser is also accountable for delivering on promises. Many past capacity-building projects and missions have been bedeviled by what local actors perceive as broken promises on the part of the interveners, including advisers. To counter the bad reputation this record has bequeathed to interventions, the effective adviser does all she can do to be accountable to the learner by conducting comprehensive needs and resource assessments, formulating achievement-based and solution-based learning objectives, and designing learning opportunities that are feasible and viable.

Specifically, the effective adviser takes great care to identify the areas in which she can contribute knowledge, skills, ideas, and information, and to state in concrete terms the nature and scope of the contribution that she can make. If an adviser identifies an area of weakness in a local system, and if the adviser lacks adequate competence in that area, she should reach out to or even put together a team of experts to work on that area. Once learning objectives have been established, they should be delivered either by the adviser or by someone whom she has carefully selected.

Being Sensitive to Trauma

While the adviser's role is not to provide psychosocial services to his counterpart, the trauma that counterparts bring along with them is likely to impact learning. The experience of conflict, especially its violence and injustice, almost invariably creates trauma, and thus the adviser should assume the existence of a level of trauma and recognize that counterparts and others may be living with a sense of uncertainty and vulnerability that is hard for a Western adviser to imagine. The adviser must be sensitive to the collective trauma that exists by choosing words carefully and not presenting ideas that ignore the reality of trauma. At the same time, the adviser should not acknowledge specific traumatic incidents or speak to individuals about the trauma they have suffered. The effective adviser avoids crafting a knowledge-transfer intervention that addresses an audience of survivors or victims (which is how most local actors will see themselves)—except perhaps in areas where extensive psychosocial programs have been administered to the population at large.

An adviser should research the nature and scope of the trauma and have an awareness of the impact of historical events on the population he is assisting, and the adviser should focus on the kind of trauma likely to have been experienced by those officials and other local actors who have to learn to contribute to an improved system. Many of the decisions that an adviser has to make about the content and methodology of the learning process should be run through the filter of trauma. The tone and the content of the knowledge-transfer process should show awareness of the trauma and the historical events that may have altered the way the counterpart perceives his environment. The language and the scope of the suggestions for alternative approaches should not only show awareness and even empathy but also teach skills that can be practiced by the audience. An audience that is severely traumatized by violence and fear may see the need only for skills and knowledge that will allow them to stop feeling victimized and/or fearful. They may not realize the potential that enhanced capacity may afford them, such as preventing further episodes that may induce more victimization and fear.

Notes

1. Muhammed Abu-Nimer, "Conflict Resolution Training in the Middle East: Lessons to Be Learned," *International Negotiation* 3 (1998): 99–116.
2. Jane Vella, *Learning to Listen, Learning to Teach: The Power of Dialogue in Educating Adults* (San Francisco: John Wiley & Sons, 2002).

8

How to Establish a
Good Relationship

NOTHING IS MORE IMPORTANT TO THE SUCCESS OF AN ADVISING mission than the development of a good relationship between the adviser and the counterpart—which is why that subject features, in one way or another, in every chapter of this book. This chapter, however, focuses solely on relationship building. It offers an in-depth look at the tools that the adviser needs to build relationships with the counterpart and other local individuals who have the potential to make the mission a success. The first half of the chapter describes the five stages of an adviser-counterpart relationship, and at each stage presents several scenarios that illustrate the correct—and the incorrect—approach for the adviser to take. The second half explores the essential elements of an effective working relationship: mutual respect, trust (of a certain kind), good rapport, cultural adaptability, language sensitivity, capable interpreters, denationalized models, and professional distance.

Developing the right kind of relationship is important for all sorts of reasons. For instance, a good relationship will help an adviser overcome the various obstacles that can stand in the way of access to the counterpart. Without access, the mission is doomed to failure; the adviser may remain in country, trying incessantly to gain access, but the lack of regular contact will make it impossible to jointly identify problems and their solutions. Security concerns, the bad reputation earned locally by previous advisers or by international

91

actors in general, a counterpart's congested schedule—a variety of reasons can impede access. But a good relationship can overcome these.

What constitutes a good relationship? The key ingredients are contained within the commonly used phrase, "a productive professional relationship." This label describes a narrow path between two pitfalls. On one side of the path is the danger of engaging the counterpart from afar and infrequently; such an arms'-length relationship gives the adviser little chance to listen to the counterpart and learn about her challenges and ideas and is likely to lead the adviser to recommend a cookie-cutter solution that is neither sustainable nor viable. On the other side of the path is the danger of becoming too close to the counterpart, forming a close personal relationship, even a friendship. An adviser who "goes native" can no longer see the boundary between the interests of the country or agency that deployed the adviser and the interests of the counterpart's country or institution.

The effective adviser, however, treads the narrow path of a productive professional relationship. She engages the counterpart and other stakeholders strategically with the goal of becoming sufficiently knowledgeable to be able to identify the most appropriate and effective solutions for the local context. This is a balancing act that requires a conscious effort to stay on the right path, to be friendly and open with local actors and yet not forget the objectives of the mission nor lose sight of the fact that competing interests are in play. It also requires the adviser to share expertise without insisting on a particular approach, instead allowing the counterpart to exercise her authority to effect change.

The Five Stages of an Advising Relationship

In order to get a firm footing on this path, the adviser should understand the different phases through which an adviser-counterpart relationship passes. There are five phases in all: (1) initial meetings with the counterpart, (2) identification and definition of the problem, (3) identification of a solution, (4) development of a plan to address the problem, and (5) implementation of the plan. These five phases are interdependent and overlapping. Indeed, the advising mission will travel back and forth between phases as it evolves, encounters changing conditions and shifting objectives, suffers setbacks, and achieves successes.

Phase 1: Initial Meetings with the Counterpart

The first meeting with the counterpart is an important opportunity for the adviser to signal that he is sensitive to the local context, understands that he does not have the authority to implement changes, is chiefly interested in learning about the issues facing the counterpart and his institution, and hopes to be able to share ideas and expertise that the counterpart will find useful. In other words, the effective adviser presents himself to the counterpart as a resource, as a fellow professional who will offer problem-solving assistance and who will *not* try to coerce or otherwise force the counterpart to adopt a specific approach. The effective adviser also demonstrates key attributes such as curiosity, a desire to learn, and a readiness to collaborate (sometimes with other advisers or sources of assistance).

In most cases, the adviser should not directly address issues of authority and legitimacy nor explicitly mention the bad reputation that prior advisers may have earned. Instead, the adviser should implicitly signal an awareness that he understands that counterparts are not always well served by their advisers.

Conveying such messages requires considerable tact and subtlety. Careless expressions at this early stage of the adviser-counterpart relationship can easily send the wrong signals and create an impression that cannot be subsequently erased. The following four examples illustrate the kinds of ways in which an adviser might introduce himself, and the kinds of responses they are likely to generate.

Example 1
ADVISER: Hello, my name is X and I am ready to make the changes necessary to make this ministry a real institution.
COUNTERPART: Hello, thank you for coming to my country. However, we have a real institution here and it functions exactly the way we want it to. No changes are necessary.

This interaction is obviously problematic. The adviser has no authority to make decisions, yet sounds as though he will usurp the counterpart's authority and position in the ministry. Furthermore, a discussion of change at this stage is premature in most cases and will offend the counterpart by suggesting that the ministry he manages is poorly run. This type of approach suggests that the adviser and the mission at large have already decided what the ministry lacks and how it needs to be restructured, and thus the adviser is uninterested in hearing the opinions of the counterpart and the ministry's staff.

Example 2
ADVISER: [Shakes the hand of the counterpart and looks him in the eye] I want to learn a lot about your country.
COUNTERPART: Thank you for your interest in my country. We have a tourist office in the town square and I encourage you to get all your information there. My cousin works there and she will take good care of you. I hope you enjoy yourself. Thank you for your visit.

Although it is not inappropriate to show interest in the host country and to signal that one wants to learn about it, the adviser is in the country to share knowledge and expertise and to assist the counterpart in solving a difficult problem. The counterpart will want to hear that the adviser understands her role and does not see herself as a tourist.

Example 3
ADVISER: Hey, I am ready to implement my very sophisticated, high-performance system from back at home.
COUNTERPART: Oh, yes, I have heard about your very sophisticated systems. I read that in your country a man was convicted and put in jail, and then you found out ten years later that he was innocent. This is a much more sophisticated system than ours. And by the way, nice to meet you, welcome to my country. Do you have a family?

This approach is likely to sound arrogant and disrespectful. It signals that the adviser will import a cookie-cutter solution, because she believes that it is the best no matter what the context in which it is applied. An adviser who exhibits this attitude becomes vulnerable to ridicule and establishes a reputation for lacking not only humility but also legitimacy as a capacity builder. Furthermore, the familiar tone ("Hey") is misplaced in a conversation between equals and professionals. The counterpart is not a friend but a respected colleague, and should be treated as such.

Example 4
ADVISER: Please, tell me about your system, how it operates, and how it translates into a service to the population.
COUNTERPART: Please sit down. Thank you for your interest in how we do things here. Can I ask you to tell me about the work that you do back at home? I have just a few minutes but I would like to schedule another meeting tomorrow with you.

This is the approach that effective advisers will choose, although each adviser will reformulate it in her own words. It shows a professional interest in learning about the ministry, not just the wider local culture, and demonstrates already that the adviser is a listener and is looking for areas in which her expertise may be useful to the counterpart, his staff, and the ministry as a whole.

Phase 2: Identification and Definition of the Problem

Once the adviser has laid the foundation for a professional relationship with the counterpart based on mutual respect for each other's experience and expertise, he must begin to promote and facilitate a dialogue to establish a joint understanding of the problem(s) that they will solve as a team. Every assumption that the adviser has about local realities and possibilities should be articulated and tested. Understanding how the counterpart defines the problem with which he needs assistance will likely be very informative. Hence, the effective adviser listens strategically and seeks to gain as comprehensive a picture as possible. The adviser can think of the problem as a puzzle with many pieces, and as each piece is placed in its correct place it reveals new information about the problem as a whole.

Sensitive to the fact that institutional weaknesses and vulnerabilities are being exposed, the counterpart may feel a little uncomfortable in this phase, and may be slow to provide pertinent information. To make the counterpart feel more relaxed, the adviser should resist any temptation to interject his own opinions and instead let the counterpart do most of the talking, thereby enabling the adviser to see the issue at hand from the local actors' perspective.

The following four examples illustrate the strengths and weaknesses of different approaches at this phase.

Example 1
ADVISER: In my predeployment briefing, I was told that you have a problem with corruption among your staff.
COUNTERPART: I don't know of a corruption problem.

This statement positions the adviser too close to the intelligence community of his country in the eyes of the counterpart. The adviser will have a difficult time establishing a productive relationship with the counterpart if he sends the message that the most valuable information comes from trusted sources back at home. Furthermore, this statement can sound like an accusation, suggesting that the ministry's leadership condones corrupt practices and may even be corrupt itself. In addition, the adviser should not try to define the problem himself but let the counterpart do so. Listening carefully to what the counterpart says about the nature and extent of the problem and about its causes will reveal data that the adviser can then analyze when developing a workable solution. That approach lays the foundation for obtaining buy-in for a solution.

Example 2
ADVISER: Okay, so I see your main problems. Don't worry; I know how to fix them.
COUNTERPART: Ah! You have been talking to my staff? And you understand our problems, as you say? Many problems we have come from the intervention from the international community, are you aware of that?

The effective adviser strives to facilitate a discussion about the issues that the counterpart and his staff face, how they see them, and how they define them. That discussion may bring up issues that the adviser did not see as a problem; it may also reveal that what the adviser does see as a problem is not perceived as such by the local actors. It is thus wise for the adviser to refrain from pointing out problems (doing so may even make local actors reluctant to accept that any problem exists) and instead focus on enabling local actors to discover problems for themselves.

Example 3

ADVISER: I would like to engage all the stakeholders to see how we can establish accountability in the department and ensure civilian oversight.

COUNTERPART: I am the only person that you need to talk to about this, as I am the person responsible for it all. All others take my orders.

Although showing a desire to engage a larger group of concerned actors in the process of change or reform is a good idea, this approach may well send the message that the authority and position of the counterpart are not as important to the adviser as they are to the counterpart. Moreover, the notion of "civilian oversight" sounds very Western; such ideas are best discussed in the solution phase, once the counterpart has accepted that a specific problem exists and a specific solution is needed.

Example 4

ADVISER: I have experience addressing issues that we may have in common. Could you tell me more about your logistics system for police equipment?

COUNTERPART: Really? You have these problems in your country also? We have several problems that I know are making us less responsive to our population's security needs. Let me tell you what they are and what we are doing to address these problems.

This approach suggests to the counterpart that the adviser can be a valuable resource, because she has experience addressing problems that the counterpart is facing. It also signals that those problems are not unique to the counterpart's institution and country; to the contrary, they are a concern for government officials in other parts of the world. This approach enables the adviser to present herself as curious rather than accusatory, and as an expert focused on a specific topic.

Phase 3: Identification of a Solution

By this phase, the astute adviser has gained an in-depth understanding of the issues, the challenges, and even some of the opportunities facing the counterpart. The adviser has likely identified common problems that different processes, systems, agencies, and even individuals have faced; and he has likely considered many ideas for tackling those problems and may even have devised an approach that seems viable and sustainable.

Now, in the third phase of the adviser-counterpart relationship, the adviser shares his knowledge and ideas, devoting a significant amount of time to explaining them, even to selling them. This is also the stage at which the effective adviser guards against taking over the project. The adviser should think of the advice he is offering as raw material for the development of solutions, but not as the solution itself.

The idea for solving the problem must come from the counterpart. The solution must be authored by those who have the authority to decide whether or not to modify, abandon, or introduce institutional processes and procedures. Solutions have to be devised and championed by local officials because identifying a solution requires an acceptance of change, which is rarely easy to do, especially when change will create losers, as is usually the case. Collective change is by definition not in everyone's interests: an effective system is one in which resources will be more evenly distributed, which means that some will have fewer resources than before.

As in phase 2, in phase 3 the effective adviser strives to promote discussion and facilitate a dialogue, but in phase 3 the content of the dialogue is the brainstorming of possible ways for the institution to move forward in a way that respects the realities on the ground. The adviser should look at the current situation; relevant past experiences; political, financial, and technological constraints; and the interests of the various stakeholders. Identifying a solution requires many consultations with the counterpart, staff, and other stakeholders, and anyone else responsible for implementing and sustaining changes. This includes future implementers, so advisers should discuss the capacities of future incoming staff with the counterpart.

The following four examples illustrate different approaches to the task of identifying a solution.

Example 1

ADVISER: At home, we do it this way, and it works every time. So let's do it.

COUNTERPART: Really? I read in the *Times* this morning that you have a problem with corruption in your ranks. . . .

Clearly, this approach is wrong in several ways. It forecloses rather than opens dialogue. It makes the adviser, not the counterpart, the leader of change. It involves a cookie-cutter solution. And it shows no respect for or understanding of the counterpart and the local context.

Example 2

ADVISER: Why don't I reach out to my colleagues back at home and get them to send me the procedure that we use in my institution so that I can put it in place for you?

COUNTERPART: Thank you, we are not used to putting procedures in place. We solve our problems by making decisions among ourselves about what would be the best way to move forward.

This approach is problematic because it fails to respect the principle of local ownership and it presumes that there are no procedures in place in the institution, suggesting that the task of looking for existing capacity has been bypassed. The adviser who reaches back to her home institution to get the model of an existing procedure that she is accustomed to using sends the signal that the adviser is not interested in looking for a local solution—and, indeed, does not believe that local ideas could be even part of a solution. The counterpart sends the signal in this scenario that, while there is decisionmaking capacity in her institution, it does not wear that Western label or follow the same path that decisionmaking travels in the adviser's home institution.

Example 3

ADVISER: What you are telling me about your system is that most components actually function well. By listening to you, I hear that the inventory capacity of your staff may sometimes contribute to less effective outcomes than you would like.

COUNTERPART: Yes, all systems are functioning. You know, the problem isn't my staff; the problem is that we have many obstacles to face and very few resources.

This statement puts the counterpart on the defensive, even if it has become evident to everyone that a problem exists and even if no one doubts its underlying cause. Calling into question the capacity of staff or the effectiveness of long-standing processes can easily sound like an accusation and may thus provoke resentment and opposition. The effective adviser shows that he understands the role that contextual factors play and the ways in which they can undermine the best efforts of a ministry's staff to develop adequate capacity.

Example 4
ADVISER: Thank you for being open and sharing some of the challenges you face. It is not always easy to do that. I would like to ask you about ideas that you may have to address the problem.
COUNTERPART: Thank you for listening. You are the first international adviser who has asked me questions that make me believe that you can help me without taking over. Here are a few ideas that I have been thinking about for a long time. Unfortunately, we have had too few resources to put these ideas into practice.

This is the approach used by the effective adviser. It shows that the adviser is opting to listen and learn, not as a visitor, but as a professional colleague who may have faced very similar situations, albeit in a different environment. This level of engagement validates the experience and expertise that the counterpart brings to the relationship and the project. This approach gives the adviser the opportunity to demonstrate empathy and respect for the challenges that the counterpart faces and has faced and to recognize that he probably has ideas about how to make positive change. The counterpart is likely to be left with the feeling that the adviser believes that the counterpart is best placed to understand the problem *and* to think of solutions that can be implemented and sustained. The adviser should ensure that he opens the door for homegrown ideas that can be implemented with the resources currently available.

Phase 4: Development of a Plan to Address the Situation

By the end of this phase, the effective adviser has a project on her hands that has been jointly designed with the counterpart and is intended to address the problem as defined and identified by the counterpart (and staff members). This phase is challenging as it requires creating a project plan, a task that is very familiar to Western experts but which tends to be very *un*familiar to government officials and their staffs in other parts of the world.

Many advisers have suggested to their counterparts the value of creating a strategic plan or specific project plan, only to find themselves drafting it. While that may be unavoidable in some instances, ideally the counterpart leads the design process. The effective adviser will ensure that the counterpart plays this role and that the staff is mobilized to support it by learning new practices. Indeed, this is an important part of the adviser's capacity-building activities and a skill to be learned and practiced often. The plan that a counterpart produces may look different from what the Western professional would draft, but that does not mean that it is an inferior plan.

Furthermore, at this phase a good adviser remembers the motto: "Be part of the process, but not the solution." In other words, developing a plan to implement a solution should be guided by the same principles that underlie the entire advising mission: promote local ownership, create sustainability, do no harm, and show respect (in this case, respect for the systems that already exist).

The following three examples illustrate three different approaches to developing a strategic plan.

Example 1
ADVISER: I know that you are very busy and have many meetings. Why don't you attend to those tasks and I will take care of drafting an implementation plan.
COUNTERPART: Okay. Please put in as much equipment as possible in your plan, because, you know, that is really all we need.

This approach violates the principle of local ownership and situates the adviser as the main architect of reform. The adviser not only lacks the authority to dictate what reforms to make but also is poorly placed to develop an adequate plan. The effective adviser recognizes that the plan is one that staffs and counterparts have to understand, implement, and maintain. A highly structured approach to reform and change (complete with sophisticated plans, precise metrics, detailed budgets, and so forth) seldom resonates in transitioning environments.

Moreover, if the adviser accedes to the counterpart's request to "put in as much equipment as possible," the adviser will be confirming the counterpart's misperception of foreign assistance as involving little or nothing more than the transfer of equipment and funds. Advising, of course, is a more abstract form of assistance in which knowledge and skills are transferred and information shared in order to establish viable and resilient practices and systems.

Example 2

ADVISER: Do I understand that your logistics manager needs skills that he does not currently possess? And do I perceive correctly that replacing her is highly problematic politically? How would you advise that we move forward in a way that your colleagues would accept?
COUNTERPART: I did not say what you claim here.

This approach is direct—probably too direct. Advocating the replacement of one of the counterpart's colleagues may strike the counterpart as an attempt by the adviser to usurp the authority to make personnel changes. If accepted, the advice may expose the counterpart to damaging repercussions from politically powerful actors and to accusations of kowtowing to foreigners. The effective adviser talks in more general terms and substantively about changing the process; she does not infringe, deliberately or inadvertently, on the counterpart's power to hire and fire.

Example 3

ADVISER: Here are my ideas. Let us adjust these in a way that would make it acceptable to your staff and your population.
COUNTERPART: Thank you for sharing your ideas and expertise with me. How can I help you adapt them to solve the problems that I shared with you earlier?

This approach is the most desirable. The adviser acknowledges that she serves as a resource and is presenting possible solutions to the counterpart so that the counterpart can decide which, if any, of those solutions to adopt or adapt. The adviser is careful to choose the word *ideas* rather than *solutions* to show that it is up to the counterpart to buy in to them or reject them.

Phase 5: Implementation of the Plan

At this final phase of the adviser-counterpart relationship, the adviser may be tempted to assume that his work is done: a plan is in place, it will be implemented, the adviser can return home. The effective adviser avoids making that assumption, however, because he is keenly aware that, having contributed to the development of a solution, he must remain on hand to help implement that solution, troubleshooting problems as they arise. Solutions that draw on ideas derived from foreign contexts have to be adapted if they are to be effective, and that process of adaptation runs more smoothly if the adviser can help tailor the idea to local circumstances. The effective adviser has been involved in the entire process of establishing a response to a problem, and is thus well placed to help the counterpart and staff overcome obstacles that threaten to block project implementation.

The following four examples illustrate different approaches an adviser can take to implementation.

Example 1

ADVISER: Let me tap my vast network to implement this for you.

COUNTERPART: This is my country and my ministry. I alone have the authority to make change. If you give me the equipment we need, I will take it from there.

The adviser is right to refrain from offering to lead or orchestrate the implementation of the plan, which is a task that the counterpart must shoulder. But the adviser is wrong to sound arrogant and oblivious to the complexities of the local environment. The adviser also makes the mistake of signaling that she is abandoning the project and leaving implementation to the counterpart, assisted by a few foreigners plucked from obscurity and expected to implement a plan that they had no part in devising. Once a trusted relationship has developed between an adviser and a counterpart, the counterpart and staff will understandably want to implement the project with the same adviser.

Example 2
ADVISER: Here are some contacts from my wide network. They can help you implement this new policy.
COUNTERPART: I prefer that we continue to work together: I trust you and we understand each other.

A good adviser refrains from passing the baton to other international actors to assist in the implementation process. After all, some of the ideas that the adviser has suggested have probably been woven into the plan for reform, and thus the adviser is uniquely well placed to help navigate through the implementation phase, making course corrections as required. Even if all of the adviser's ideas have been rejected, he has nonetheless been personally involved in facilitating the identification of both the problem and the solution, and his continued involvement will be valuable. To be sure, the adviser can and should facilitate the introduction of other experts who could be helpful, but he should remain a broker of ideas and expertise. Sharing contacts can be helpful to a counterpart, but it is a supplementary benefit; the key contribution remains the adviser himself.

Example 3
ADVISER: If you think I can be of any use, just call me.
COUNTERPART: Oh, okay—you aren't coming back?

This approach, while not intrusive and showing that the adviser recognizes that he is not in charge, does not suggest that he understands the importance of actively participating in the implementation phase.

Example 4
ADVISER: I think that you have developed a great plan. I would like to roll up my sleeves and support you in any way that you see fit.
COUNTERPART: Thank you for helping me to find the adequate solution for our ministry and our logistics system. Can you come back tomorrow at the same time so that we can start?

This approach will enable the adviser to remain involved and contribute to the project throughout the implementation phase.

The Essential Elements of a Productive Professional Relationship

Mutual Respect

Acting appropriately and effectively at each of the five stages of the adviser-counterpart relationship is impossible unless the adviser has established amicable relationships with her counterpart and members of the institution's staff that are based on mutual respect for what each brings to the table as a professional.

The effective adviser establishes a peer-to-peer relationship with her counterpart from the very first time they meet. The adviser's claim to legitimacy in the mission is her specific expertise. However, the adviser must never forget that her presence does not imply that the counterpart has no expertise. For example, both the adviser and the counterpart may be technical experts on budgetary issues. And both may track spending in similar ways or at least for similar reasons, albeit in very different contexts. Acknowledging the fact that both have some technical expertise and knowledge to offer is the first step toward building a peer-to-peer relationship.

Both the adviser and the counterpart have specific strengths—ideally, distinct yet complementary strengths—to bring to the project. The adviser

- offers lessons learned from prior experiences in problem-solving efforts;
- acts as a catalyst, promoting linkages between individuals, institutions, and even issues;
- brings in an outsider's opinion on a particular subject and the ability to inspire thinking outside the box;
- acts as a sounding board, allowing counterparts to voice opinions and concerns and discuss possible consequences; and
- serves as a bridge for importing good international practice into the host country or institution.

The counterpart

- brings important local knowledge about culture, history, and political context;
- offers insight into the structure and functioning of the host institution;
- provides information about and explanations of specific issues, or can tell the adviser who to turn to for such information; and
- vets proposals for cultural acceptability and economic and political viability.

The effective adviser defines the counterpart as both the advisee and the adviser. The counterpart receives technical expertise and knowledge to enhance her ability to envision, plan, and implement reform activities; advisers receive guidance on a foreign environment and culture.

A Certain Kind of Trust

There is much discussion about trust and building trust in adviser circles. The adviser has to establish trust with the counterpart, so the thinking goes, if the adviser is to accomplish her mission. But what kind of "trust" are we talking about? "Trust" is a very personal concept; some of us trust easily, and others require their trust to be earned over a long time. And can trust ever really be built between individuals with very different approaches, experiences, and beliefs about what trust looks like in a relationship?

Instead of trying to answer these intractable questions, the effective adviser focuses on developing a very particular, very instrumental kind of trust: *trust in the adviser's expertise and its relevance to the issue that the counterpart is addressing.* In other words, the effective adviser seeks to gain the trust of the counterpart in the value of the adviser's knowledge and ideas. "Trust" that extends further than this may not be attainable, and thus the dogged pursuit of such trust may be a waste of the adviser's time and effort.

In some instances, advisers define trust in the context of personal safety: the adviser trusts the counterpart not to harm the adviser and/or to work to ensure the safety of the adviser. Trusting your counterpart in this physical sense may involve, for instance, walking in front of her without fear of being attacked by the counterpart. This kind of trust is very different, of course, from trust that the counterpart is sharing accurate and complete information relevant to capacity building.

Good Rapport

Mutual respect is vital, but by itself it cannot protect a relationship against the inevitable ups and downs of capacity-building activities. To create relationships that can weather adversity, an adviser needs to spend a lot of time building rapport. From an adviser's perspective, "rapport" means a working relationship that is shaped by harmony, common ground, communication, and flexibility. The adviser lacks official authority and cannot foster change or transfer knowledge without the voluntary participation of local actors; securing that kind of participation requires developing a rapport with key officials and stakeholders.

One of the first tasks of an adviser is to build rapport. Advisers who have practiced exhaustively their rapport-building skills before deployment can hit the ground running.

Building rapport can be thought of as a process with three key components: introducing the adviser as a resource; working with individuals with different social styles; and listening actively to identify solutions.

Introducing the adviser as a resource. An adviser engages the counterpart strategically from the very beginning by introducing herself as an expert who can be useful to the individuals addressing a problem in their institution. Rather than focusing on her other identities (e.g., nationality, religion, ethnicity), the adviser emphasizes her identity as an expert in a field relevant to the work of the institution. Thus, when meeting the counterpart for the first time, the effective adviser can succinctly explain who she is and what her specific mission is, and then quickly move on to an "elevator speech." An elevator speech is very concise (no more than five sentences) and signals an adviser's understanding of her role and the task at hand. It paves the way for a peer-to-peer working relationship based on mutual respect for each other's identity as a professional expert in, say, the delivery of vaccines or the recruitment of police officers. An elevator speech is necessary because an adviser may not be able to schedule a long meeting with a busy counterpart, and thus the adviser needs to swiftly deliver the message that she is there in a supportive, expert role.

In preparing to meet with the counterpart for the first time, the adviser should ask herself the following questions:

- What is my specific mission?
- What are my unique assets?
- How do I fit in? In what capacity can I solve problems?
- What types of problems have I addressed in my career that are likely to plague the counterpart's institution?
- How do I present myself as a resource, someone without formal authority but with useful expertise?
- How do I show that I will operate as a peer?

Working with individuals with different social styles. The adviser needs to build a rapport with more than one person. The adviser may have several counterparts, or he may have only one counterpart but need to develop relationships with a variety of influential local actors. Each of these individuals will have a distinctive social style, and the adviser must tailor his rapport-building approach to fit these different styles.

Customizing approaches is necessary even when the adviser is building relationships in a familiar environment. It acquires yet more importance in a culture, an institution, and a country with which the adviser is unfamiliar. Fortunately, there is a vast body of knowledge on assessing an interlocutor that can be helpful for an adviser.[1] This literature can sharpen an adviser's awareness of the social styles of others (e.g., how they receive information and the body language they employ) and of the adviser's own social style. Above all, the adviser must know how to interact with other social styles.

Among the various social style frameworks that can be found in the literature, the ACES model is very useful for the adviser who is attempting to establish a productive professional relationship with a counterpart.[2] The ACES model allows the adviser to identify the type of information and the topics of conversation which will be of most interest to the counterpart. This model differentiates among four social styles (the first letters of which spell out "ACES"): analytical, commander, expressive, and stabilizer.

An individual who possesses the *analytical* style seeks data, accuracy, and analysis. He is organized, detail-oriented, idealistic, easily disappointed, moody, and sarcastic. The analytical individual is likely to dress conservatively, exhibit a closed posture (e.g., crossed arms), and keep his work area orderly. He speaks in a measured tone and volume, and emphasizes facts.

The *commander* is the style of people who seek control, tend to be high achievers, and are bold and assertive. They are sometimes referred to as "natural leaders," and exhibit competitive, egocentric, and headstrong behavior. Commanders are also known for having relatively short tempers. They can be identified by their dress, which commands power and respect (their quintessential attire in the West is the "power suit"). They tend to get physically close to those with whom they are talking and speak rapidly and loudly, eager to discover the bottom line or get to the "point."

A very different style is exhibited by *expressive* individuals, who are social, enjoy interacting with others, and seek pleasant experiences. They are animated, cheerful, talkative, and generally enthusiastic and lacking in discipline. They usually dress flamboyantly. Their workspaces contain gadgets, even toys. They speak rapidly and loudly, laugh a good deal, and try to get physically close to their interlocutor.

An individual who exhibits the *stabilizer* style seeks order and stability. The stabilizer tends to be accommodating, considerate, and easygoing, and to avoid conflict at any cost. Stabilizers are likely to have closed postures. They speak slowly and softly, and they prefer to talk first about leisure time and family before moving on to business. They employ terms such as "help," "team," and "working together."

Each of these social styles has its strengths and weaknesses but, from the adviser's perspective, what is important is to identify which style an individual possesses as well as his own style to determine how to best interact with the counterpart. The effective adviser does this by picking up visual and oral social clues and building a profile of an individual. Armed with this knowledge, the adviser will be better able to develop a rapport, bridge communication gaps between individuals with different styles, and not let differing approaches to decisionmaking, discussion, and debate limit the effectiveness of the project. For example, if an adviser's style is analytical, and he identifies the counterpart as a commander, the adviser will have to refocus his attention much closer toward the bottom line—the final result of a project—and pay less attention to the facts and figures that support the project. Similarly, a stabilizer counterpart will not respond well to a commander adviser unless the adviser can make his style seem less aggressive and pushy.

Listening actively to identify solutions. The effective adviser spends a lot of time identifying the issues that contribute to the gaps in capacity that plague a specific system. This is difficult work because a complex and interdependent set of systems, processes, practices, and dynamics are in play, and these can be understood only through careful, conscious, and patient listening. Briefings and other information that the adviser receives during predeployment training are helpful when they can be used to formulate informed questions throughout the advising mission. However, briefings of any kind from any source can serve only as the preliminary foundation for an understanding of a specific situation involving specific individuals and specific practices. That in-depth understanding must be built by an adviser who is expert in the specific field and who has the opportunity to ask pertinent questions and listen carefully to what counterparts and staff say in response. For example, an experienced logistics professional who has significant expertise in solving problems and managing logistics systems is best equipped to ask a counterpart and staff the most pertinent questions about gaps in local logistical capacity—questions whose answers will help that professional develop an in-depth understanding of the local system.

Listening strategically means acquiring information that leads to a comprehensive understanding of the pros and cons of a system. It also means asking the right questions. Questions are most conducive to the sharing of information when they are formulated in ways that are neither judgmental, nor accusatory, nor suggestive of blame or shame. The effective adviser takes great care to formulate questions in a way that will engage rather than deter local actors. (See Chapter 5 for a discussion of how to frame questions.)

To ensure that she understands what the counterpart says in response, the effective adviser will restate the information and knowledge that she has gained from each exchange. In other words, the adviser explains how, based on what the counterpart has said, the adviser sees the problem, the interests at stake, and the dynamics in play. Then, the adviser and the counterpart can discuss challenges and possible consequences of the ways forward being considered. This gives the counterpart options. The adviser should also ask many questions about the viability and sustainability of the proposed solution. A discussion of all possible ramifications—positive and negative—of proposed changes should occur, and stakeholders whose opinions have not yet been solicited should be consulted.

Cultural Adaptability

Conventional wisdom dictates that *cultural awareness* is very important for an adviser, as it is for anyone working in a foreign environment. And, indeed, an adviser does need to be aware that local norms, habits, practices, and assumptions differ from those found in the adviser's society. For example, a culturally aware adviser assisting a ministry of interior in a conservative society would recognize that special accommodations have to be made to recruit, train, and manage women police officers. Equally, a culturally aware adviser working in a society in which interpersonal relationships form the basis for business relationships would recognize the wisdom of accepting offers to dinner and other social engagements. But this level of cultural sensitivity awareness is not enough for strategic advisers. They must move beyond cultural awareness and develop *cultural adaptability,* which will allow them to see options in foreign environments that would not look like options in their own cultural contexts.

The strategic adviser adapts to cultural norms by understanding that culture affects how people conceive of their world and by learning about the various components that make cross-cultural engagements successful. For example, an adviser should understand that different cultures have different attitudes toward time. Some focus on the future, others are more concerned about the past; some value precise schedules and promptness, others prefer flexible schedules and do not take lateness personally. Similarly, attitudes toward authority can vary markedly. Some cultures emphasize hierarchy and tradition but also prefer to negotiate with people with whom they have developed personal ties; other cultures tolerate much greater individuality and encourage creativity but are happy to do business with people with whom they have no social connections.[3]

Cultural adaptability allows the adviser to put her cultural awareness to work for them. A culturally adaptable adviser is able to form her own analysis of the cultural components in play in a specific situation and then identify which of the adviser's own practices and ideas need to be adapted to fit the situation. For example, in a culture (whether social and/or institutional) that prizes hierarchy, an adviser who is about to launch a training program within a ministry should always give the official in charge the chance to instruct his staff to attend that training.

A culturally *aware* adviser might know that recruiting women into the police is controversial locally. A culturally *adaptable* adviser, however, would not simply abandon the idea of recruiting women but would instead identify steps that can be taken around the cultural obstacles in the path of female police officers. The adviser might propose building separate facilities for women and training women separately. The adviser might also find ways to persuade local people to view female police officers as culturally desirable—for instance, the adviser might argue that addressing crimes against women is best done by women police officers.

Cultural adaptability is very important in building rapport. The effective adviser understands the ways in which cultural differences can affect relationship building and strives to identify approaches that are culturally acceptable. For example, strategic planning is the foundation and the guiding light of most reform efforts in liberal, Western societies. But the very formal and highly inclusive process of strategic planning is not the norm in more conservative societies in which a few individuals make decisions for the many. Building rapport with the counterpart rests on the ability of the adviser to propose ideas that sound viable to the counterpart.

Language Sensitivity

Just as cultural adaptability is a rapport-building tool, language sensitivity can also build bridges. Being sensitive to language is not the same as being able to speak a foreign language. Being sensitive to language means recognizing that language is a tool to communicate ideas, and that the nature of those ideas can be shaped by the language used to express them. Each language has its own unique mode of sending messages, using expressions laden with history and culture, and deploying idioms and metaphors that are usually a lot less transparent than they seem to native speakers. To take a very simple example: some languages and cultures make extensive use of sporting metaphors to describe conflicts—but those metaphors implicitly present conflict as governed by rules, like a sporting contest. For people from other cultures, this equation of conflict and sport may seem preposterous or bewildering. Language sensitivity will enable an adviser to see through the metaphor to the concept and the assumptions that lie behind it.

An adviser who can speak a few words of the local language should not assume that he thus has the key to understanding local problems. This is not to downplay the value of an adviser being able to speak his counterpart's language fluently. But one must be truly fluent to dispense with the services of an interpreter. Institution building involves numerous complicated issues (from corruption to procurement to gender mainstreaming), each of which tends to have its own technical lexicon and linguistic nuances. Furthermore, technical words in one language may have no parallel in another; for instance, concepts and technologies that are common in one country but have yet to penetrate another country will have names in the former country's language but not in the latter's. In most cases, the adviser needs an interpreter to communicate with counterparts.

Even minimal language skills are useful, however. In the first place, some language proficiency demonstrates to a counterpart that the adviser has made an effort to learn the counterpart's language—and thus to respect the counterpart's culture. To be able to begin a meeting with a few sentences in the local language requires work but it can help to establish a bond. A second benefit of acquiring some basic local language skills is the ability to work with an interpreter more effectively. Understandably, interpreters can find it difficult to accurately convey the meaning of highly technical terminology and concepts. It is thus useful for an adviser to build a lexicon of key terms in his area of expertise, and to know the spelling and pronunciation of each term in the local language. This knowledge will allow the adviser to check the accuracy, at least to some degree, of what his interpreter says to the counterpart; it will also let the adviser pick up some hints about what the counterpart is telling the interpreter.

Capable Interpreters

Recruiting, selecting, contracting, and developing an effective working relationship with an interpreter are key advising skills. The effective adviser understands interpreting to be the art of making meaning. Interpretation is often erroneously believed to be the process of identifying words that have the closest equivalent in another language. Increasingly, however, interpreters are being recognized as "cultural advisers," a term that describes a key aspect of interpreting. In cases in which ideas are new to an environment, word-for-word interpretation may not be appropriate, and the interpreter may have to demonstrate ingenuity and flexibility in conveying the idea in terms that local people can understand

Selecting an interpreter takes time and significant effort.[4] An interpreter should be well versed in both the adviser's language and the counterpart's language (and in dialects spoken by influential local actors) and should also understand the basic culture of both societies. Candidates for the job of interpreter should be carefully interviewed to ascertain their qualifications and vetted for impartiality by contacting references and reading their service records (if they exist). The adviser must ask a candidate specific questions about her familiarity with the subject matter, knowledge of the local or institutional environment, and other situational factors. An interpreter may perform perfectly in one situation but lack the competence to function even adequately in another.

Identity issues matter when choosing interpreters. Markers of identity such as nationality, ethnicity, religion, tribe, clan, or even political affiliation can significantly influence the interpreter's ability to communicate effectively on behalf of the adviser. An interpreter whose identity creates problems of trust, credibility, and even access to local actors will be a handicap for the adviser.

The adviser should treat the interpreter as part of the team—a team member whose duty is to ensure clear communication. When the adviser addresses large audiences, the interpreter should stand next to the adviser; when the adviser talks to a single individual, the interpreter should form a triangle by standing midway between the two interlocutors but to one side. The effective adviser engages her interlocutor directly, making eye contact and making sure her body language sends the right message to the interlocutor. The interpreter is not the audience, but a member of the team that is sending the message. And as a team member, she should not be spoken over. The adviser should speak slowly, pause frequently, and give the interpreter the time to formulate the entire message accurately and completely.

In preparing for an event, a discussion, or even a working relationship, the adviser should work with the interpreter, rehearsing where the interpreter will stand or sit, checking that the interpreter has done her background reading, ensuring that the tone and pitch of the interpreter's voice are appropriate, and explaining technical terms. The adviser should also consider bringing a note taker to the meeting, so that the material exchanged between interlocutor and adviser can be reviewed and any misunderstandings can be corrected.

Denationalized Models and Solutions

Most practices that advisers know well have evolved in their home countries to fit the particular conditions—cultural, historical, legal, technical, and so forth—of that country. As a consequence, some practices cannot be transferred from one country to another, and other practices can be transferred only in part. The effective adviser takes great care then to identify which parts of his expertise are system- or culture-specific and which parts are not.

For example, a US police officer should not teach a police counterpart in a host country to read the "Miranda" rights of a suspect, because those rights apply only under the US legal code. But that does not mean that the adviser cannot share the idea underlying the Miranda rights with local police officials who are interested in deciding if and how to inform suspects of their rights.

Another example of the need to denationalize models concerns internal audits. An internal audit process is one in which measures are taken to ensure compliance with the policies and procedures of an institution. This process has evolved over time in Western countries, becoming embedded in the principles of accountability, transparency, and efficiency—all Western conceptualizations of control of the behavior of individuals and institutions. But internal audits are still a very foreign process in many transitioning societies, where audits would be seen as highly invasive and likely to embarrass officials by exposing certain activities and behavior. The effective adviser will thus introduce the idea of "control" rather than of an "internal audit." Control is a much more widely understood concept, and it can be discussed without having to recount the historical development of a sophisticated, specific process. Controls that fit the local perpective can be instituted.

Professional Distance

While becoming adaptable and open to learning new habits and customs is laudable, the effective adviser guards against "going native." Going native describes a process in which advisers lose their professional distance; they stop seeing themselves as part of the broader mission and as a temporary support to local actors, and instead identify themselves with the counterpart, adopting, rather than adapting to, the counterpart's interests. Advisers who go native may adopt the dress and grooming practices of local actors and/or they may assimilate the outlook and defend the interests of local actors. ("Change," they may say, "is not in the interest of my counterpart.") The outward signs of going native are less threatening to the integrity of the advising mission than the inward shift in outlook.

Advisers who adopt the views and methods of counterparts and their institutions lose their perspective as problem solvers and become a liability for their mission. They become adept at seeing the problems that counterparts face, but they relinquish their ability to diagnose problems and identify possible solutions. The effective adviser remains an outsider who remembers that he is a resource for local actors.

Notes

1. See, for example, William Snavely and Ellen Walters, "Differences in Communication Competence in Administrative Social Styles," *Journal of Applied Communication Research* 11, no. 2 (1983); Robert Bolton and Dorothy Grover Bolton, *Social Style–Management Style: Developing Productive Work Relationships* (New York: Amacom, 1984); Norman Fairclough, "Critical Discourse Analysis," in *How to Analyse Talk in Institutional Settings* (Bodmin, UK: MPG Book Ltd., 2001), 25–40.

2. Michael Beck, "The 5 Mistakes Executives Most Often Make (and How to Avoid Them)," Executive Briefing, October 2005, Denver, CO.

3. Richard H. Solomon and Nigel Quinney, *American Negotiating Behavior: Wheeler-Dealers, Legal Eagles, Bullies, and Preachers* (Washington, DC: United States Institute of Peace Press, 2010), 48–55.

4. This section is drawn from Dominic Kiraly, "Making Meaning Through Interpreters: Lessons Learned in Zones of Conflict," USIP instruction CD (2011), available by request from USIP Publications.

9

Coordinating with Other Actors

INTERNATIONAL INTERVENTIONS ARE INVARIABLY HIGHLY COM-
plex undertakings, with many different types of actors from many
different countries and organizations working in the same arena.
Coordinating their work is very difficult, but a failure to coordinate
will result in competition, confusion, duplication of effort, and the
very real possibility that little capacity will be built and even less
sustained.

An adviser, of course, cannot coordinate an entire international
intervention, but she can try to coordinate efforts within her own
sphere of activity. For instance, an adviser can seek to foster cooperation among the various actors trying to build capacity within a particular sector of the national government or a particular ministry. The
task is likely to seem daunting, but sometimes beginning the process
is the hardest part. Once the adviser understands that some coordination is achievable, she is likely to be less anxious about the fact that
not everything in a foreign environment can be coordinated.

Coordination is variously defined. One definition particularly
appropriate for the advising mission comes from the field of business. It holds that, in essence, coordination is the act of managing
interdependencies between activities that are designed to achieve a
particular goal[1]—even if, as in the case of international interventions,
the goals of the actors are rarely articulated in such a way as to form
an explicit common goal.

119

This short chapter examines the task of coordination from an adviser's perspective. It first notes the main obstacles to coordination in crowded and complex arenas and sketches some of the different types of actors found in most missions. The chapter then outlines some practical steps that an adviser can take toward making coordination a reality.[2]

Obstacles to Coordination

The failure to coordinate can have dire consequences. An inability to coordinate can lead to wasteful duplication of efforts, either because of ignorance (e.g., one actor launches a program to fill a gap, not knowing that another actor is already running a program intended to plug that gap) or because of a lack of trust (e.g., one actor refuses to share information about his activities with other actors, fearful that they will use that information to undermine, inadvertently or deliberately, his work). A lack of coordination can also often lead to negative interactions with institutions with whom the adviser should be partnering and whose specialized expertise the adviser should be incorporating into his work. In extreme cases, the failure to coordinate can even lead to mission failure.

Thus, the effective adviser actively seeks to encourage coordination whenever and wherever possible and establishes mechanisms to share information with others who have the potential to enhance or threaten the adviser's activities. This, however, is easier said than done.

It is no secret that coordination with widely diverse actors is difficult to achieve. Goals, activities, and mission caveats can differ profoundly even among actors funded by the same government. After more than ten years of capacity-building efforts in Afghanistan, lack of coordination among international actors on civil service reform and the civilianization of security ministries produced a civil service that was unable to perform the duties required of it in the two main security ministries. Some promising efforts in Afghanistan have been undone by a lack of resources; others, by a tangle of multiple funding streams. Afghan law enforcement institutions and various forces have been developed along conceptual and legal lines that are tied to the nationalities of the funding sources—Germany, then the United

States, and now increasingly the European Union Law. The result has been inefficiency and disjointed development of different law enforcement capacities, and these have delayed the creation of an effective system of law enforcement in Afghanistan.

Advisers often have to interact with a number of organizations in the field that are structured very differently than the adviser's own and have very different organizational cultures. In some organizations, efforts to coordinate with other actors may be directed from above and may be required to follow specific procedures, rules, and regulations. Other organizations may encourage lower-level staff to launch their own initiatives to coordinate, and to do so in flexible, adaptable ways. While some organizations may have a clearly defined person responsible for orchestrating coordination, others may have no one tasked with that job. For instance, NGOs working in conflict zones typically are "flat" organizations (i.e., their hierarchies are highly compressed) with few personnel, each of whom wears a lot of different hats, so their personnel may not have the time to coordinate with the adviser, or the adviser may find it difficult to identify a contact within the NGO. Even a single organization may consist of separate entities, each with its own hierarchical and bureaucratic structures and culture. Many field offices have a number of different offices, each focusing on a different aspect of the overall capacity-building effort, which can make it very difficult for the adviser to determine which office he should be or could be working with.

Some organizations are even prohibited by their own regulations from working with certain other organizations. For example, most NGOs have policies that bar them from interacting with the military (e.g., riding in military convoys) to avoid being perceived by the local community as a partner of the military, which may be seen locally as a source of danger rather than protection. NGOs usually depend on their ties to the local communities for their safety.

The environment in which the adviser has to operate is very dynamic, making it difficult for development actors, security actors, NGOs, and international organizations to coordinate their diverse activities. For instance, one province of the country may have escaped much of the fighting and be relatively stable, and thus development organizations are leading most initiatives in that area, leaving the security institutions to play a secondary or even tertiary role there. But in another province in the same country, violent conflict may still be ongoing or spoilers may be trying to reignite the conflict, and thus security actors are taking the lead in that area. Trying to coordinate between security and development actors in such an uneven, fluctuating environment can be extremely difficult.

Complex Environments, Multiple Actors

The missions in which advisers serve often have three layers of complexity—and advisers are virtually certain to encounter at least the second and third of these.[3]

One layer of complexity consists of the security threats present in postconflict, transitioning countries. Insurgents pose security threats, of course, but so do a multitude of actors who stand to lose from reform and enhanced government capacity. A second layer emerges from the weakness of the state and the government: a governance structure that is riddled with gaps. And a third layer is made up of the multitude of actors involved in a host country. Even in interventions far more limited in scope than the missions in Iraq and Afghanistan, the adviser will almost certainly not be the only international actor on the ground—and those international actors will be working alongside or otherwise interacting with a host of local actors.

The following five types of actors are usually present in transitioning societies:

• *The international community.* The community of donor countries will be present in both a multilateral and a unilateral form. Multilateral arrangements can themselves take many forms, such as ad hoc coalitions formed specifically for the purpose of intervening in the host country, as well as long-standing regional organizations that have deployed personnel to the country to help with the transition. Many individual countries are also likely to be on the scene. In some instances, a country's representatives will be embedded within a regional organization; in other cases, they will form a stand-alone mission that is run out of their country's embassy and that funds and administers programs and projects that are important to the country's government. For instance, a US country team might include USAID program officers, Department of State bureau program officers, and Federal Bureau of Investigation (FBI) trainers.

These national actors often develop specialized expertise over the course of years spent working in similar environments. For example, New Zealand has significant expertise in running detention facilities, Norway focuses its efforts on development and humanitarian assistance, and Canada has an excellent track record of supporting local police forces.

• *International organizations.* A host of international organizations, each with its own specific mandate from its member states, may be on the scene. Some will have a relatively narrow focus: the mandate of the International Committee of the Red Cross, for instance, is "ensuring humanitarian protection and assistance for victims of war and armed violence." Others have a much broader agenda: the United Nations Development Programme (UNDP), for example, works in such diverse areas as poverty reduction, human rights, democratic governance, and crisis prevention.

The UN can seem a rather confusing organization to deal with at first, because it has many different organizations within it. The UN's development arm includes such entities as the United Nations Children's Fund (UNICEF), the World Health Organization (WHO), and the UNDP. Its main security institution is the United Nations Department of Peacekeeping Operations (UNDPKO), which oversees and supports the many UN peacekeeping missions. To further complicate matters, in most missions the UN's most visible figure to the host government will be an SRSG (a special representative of the UN secretary-general), appointed specifically to meet with heads of state and represent the organization in various ways, both public and private.

• *Regional actors.* Regional actors are increasingly involved in the negotiations to transition a country from war to peace. Many of these regional organizations, such as the African Union, have a security arm, and troops from that entity may be in the country to help implement the political programs that negotiations have yielded. Regional organizations are also likely to have offices in the country that focus on peace building and development. They typically staff their offices with both international and local staff, who work with local counterparts in their respective sectors.

• *Local officials and elites.* In addition to her counterpart, the adviser will encounter, directly or indirectly, many other government officials from the host country. Despite all being part of the same government, they are highly unlikely to share the same attitude toward capacity-building missions, and the adviser should distinguish between supporters and opponents.

High-ranking officials are typically drawn from the ranks of the nation's elite, but the adviser's work may also bring her into contact with members of the elite and other local leaders who are not part of the government, such as religious leaders or prominent members of civil society organizations. These individuals can hold significant power within their community and influence its readiness to accept or reject change and reform, especially when reform is being promoted by a government with little legitimacy or by outside actors. For example, elites may use their influence to shape how the mass media (through editorials, talk radio shows, and so forth) portray the problems facing a society and the merits of different options for tackling them.

• *Civil society.* Civil society actors are very important for knitting together citizens and their government. Civil society actors range from religious organizations and charities to universities, media outlets, and professional organizations. Their capacity and leverage is often greater than it might first appear to the adviser. Failing to engage civil society organizations threatens the sustainability of any reform effort. As a general rule, civil society actors are less interested in which personalities will occupy high-ranking government positions and more interested in the processes of governance that will allow the population to engage its government during and after the transition.

Each of these actors has the potential to intersect with, compete with, complicate, undermine, or complement the adviser's own work. For example, human rights training conducted by NGOs may set the tone for subsequent efforts by the adviser to nurture respect for human rights among members of the security forces. Similarly, civil society organizations that monitor the security services can help to foster a climate in which the police and army feel obliged to respect human rights laws.

The adviser should thus first identify the other actors sharing the same space in the host country and then determine their agendas, interests, resources, power relations, and activities. It is useful to identify the interdependencies between these actors and the adviser's own activities. The multiplicity of actors and, at times, the lack of clarity regarding their mandates and activities will make it difficult to see the links between various programs. But highlighting interdependencies may encourage those concerned to coordinate with each other, exchange good practices and lessons learned, avoid duplication, and spotlight potential partners and resources.

Promoting Coordination

Armed with this information, the adviser can promote coordination in various ways. She can foster the development of a shared understanding of the problems in the environment, establish a team to coordinate efforts to address those problems, identify common priorities and objectives, and map each party's contribution to addressing the problem.[4]

Developing a Shared Understanding and Establishing a Team

Many of the obstacles to coordination discussed above arise because of the different perspectives from which the various international actors address an issue. Therefore, the first step for the adviser is to encourage the development of a shared understanding of the problems in the environment. Joint analysis does not mean that all players view the problems in exactly the same way; rather, joint analysis allows parties to educate, inform, and learn from each other's different vantage points. Coming to a common understanding means that players have the opportunity to explain the issues they face and present their opinion on the impact of these issues on the ability of the system (i.e., the institution) to function effectively.

A shared understanding of a problem requires the sharing of information, assessments, and individual analyses of the problem. This is a gradual process. The participation of all or most of the relevant actors will take time to achieve, because of busy schedules, a lack of interest in or understanding of the need for coordination, or a lack of willingness to share information. Nevertheless, the adviser should still initiate discussion, even with a very small group. As meetings become better attended and a clear focus is articulated, other actors in the environment will want to join and contribute. Where possible, the adviser should invite the counterpart to either lead the coordination efforts or identify another appropriate local actor to lead.

Information-seeking questions can be a useful tool in building a shared understanding of common problems. Each member of the coordinating group could be asked such questions as:

- How do you see the problem that we're working on?
- What has shifted in the ministry that may change how we think about this particular project?
- What is your organization's assessment of what is going on in terms of project implementation?
- Do you see any problems ahead?

Discussing the relevant issues in this manner allows all involved to understand the situation in a new light, which paves the way for the development of a common set of objectives and even a group identity. The adviser gains valuable insight from this process—principally, an understanding of the dynamics that affect the counterpart and his institution.

Identifying Common Priorities and Objectives

Once a shared understanding of the problem, or at least some aspects of the problem, has been established, common priorities and objectives can be identified. It is important that all feel that they are advancing their respective agencies' missions. For example, the adviser who is working to support the development of a logistics management system in a defense ministry can encourage those working on equipment donations to structure deliveries in accordance with the new system. In this way, the adviser is fulfilling his role to enhance the capacity of the defense ministry, and the organization that manages equipment transfers ensures that the items are efficiently received, inventoried, secured, and distributed. Both parties have a common interest: to ensure military operations are adequately equipped.

Many other aspects of equipment transfer are also interdependent and serve the common interest, including security during delivery, procurement and contracting, maintenance and distribution, and retention of the equipment. One capacity-building effort will thus depend on many others occurring simultaneously. But common interests and common objectives can be difficult to see when players are narrowly focused on their own tasks. A forum for discussion allows the bigger picture to come into focus and reduces the risk that one player's activities will undermine another's efforts.

Identifying Each Party's Contribution and Establishing a Strong Group Identity

Once there is agreement on priorities and common objectives, there can be a discussion about what each group member brings to the table. The group can create an action plan that outlines specific roles and responsibilities for each member to ensure that any one change enhances rather than impairs others' reform efforts. These roles and responsibilities should be specified as early as possible in order to avoid confusion and duplication at a later stage.

Once these concrete discussions are under way, it is important to establish a strong identity as a group or a network. This will provide continuity to the effort and help build relationships among all members. The structure of the group is best when it is horizontal, rather than hierarchical. After all, coordination depends on voluntary collaboration and sharing of information, because no one member of the group supersedes the others in authority. Even so, a leadership component is necessary to keep the group structured and to maintain regular meetings. Therefore, it is best to appoint a lead coordinator who will engage with all members, ensure timely implementation of the action plan, and facilitate communication within and outside of the group. Again, the counterpart should be encouraged to take this role, not only addressing local ownership, but smoothing over the unavoidable political sensitivities.

Notes

1. G. M. Olson, T. W. Malone, and J. B. Smith, eds., *Coordination Theory and Collaboration Technology* (Mahwah, NJ: Erlbaum, 2001).
2. This chapter draws upon the work of Lauren Van Metre, a senior pro-

gram officer at United States Institute of Peace (USIP) who has spent years researching and teaching about obstacles to coordination.

3. Jeremiah S. Pam, "The Paradox of Complexity: Embracing Its Contribution to Situational Understanding, Resisting Its Temptation in Strategy and Operational Plans," in *Complex Operations: NATO at War and on the Margins of War,* ed. Christopher M. Schnaubelt, NATO Defense College Forum Paper no. 14 (Rome: NATO Defense College, Research Division, July 2010).

4. Lauren Van Metre, content from a USIP training course entitled "Leading Adaptive Teams in Conflict Environments," see http://www.usip.org/events/leading-adaptive-teams-in-conflict-environments.

10

How to Create Sustainability

ADVISERS HELP GOVERNMENTS DEVELOP THE CAPACITY TO MAN-
age conflicts over state resources and services. Such conflicts are
inevitable, even in stable environments. The key to preventing old
conflicts from reigniting and new ones from erupting is sustainability. Sustainable capacity building requires the adviser to assist an
institution in adapting its systems and practices to meet the demands
of constantly evolving environments. The goal of the adviser is to
contribute to the development of dynamic solutions to both chronic
and emerging problems and, when the adviser's deployment ends, to
leave the institution able to implement those solutions and to devise
new ones as circumstances demand. The effective adviser supports
change but refrains from becoming a pillar of the new system or
practice that change introduces. If the adviser, whose deployment in-
country is inevitably temporary, renders himself indispensable, the
system or practice will collapse when the adviser leaves the scene.

Donor countries have invested heavily in capacity-building missions, but unfortunately some of these investments have failed to yield
long-term benefits because foreign interventions have not recognized
the value of sustainability. The goal of any advising mission is, or
should be, to leave behind a system and a set of practices that will
become part of the structure of the institution and translate into an
enhanced government service to a targeted population. In the absence
of sustainable solutions and changes, however, this goal will never be

reached and international investments will be squandered. A number of recent interventions have defined their mission in terms of accomplishing certain national security–related objectives instead of defining it as the building of capacity; this focus is understandable but counterproductive, because unless capacity is built, solutions will not be sustainable and conflicts will reignite—and thus national security goals such as the creation of a stable, peaceful state will not be met.

Essentially, sustainability is about making change stick. This book has shown how effective advising can build capacity, but how can we be confident that the changes that the adviser and her counterpart have initiated will last? The term "sustainable development" often calls to mind technologies and policies intended to spur economic growth without inflicting long-term environmental damage, but "sustainable development" can refer to any type of lasting change. This chapter lays out information for advisers about how to promote sustainable development within government institutions.

This chapter is divided into three sections. The first spotlights some of the major obstacles to the development of sustainable systems and solutions and focuses on one particular impediment: a lack of time. The second section—the longest of the three sections—identifies six key principles that, if respected, will help an adviser overcome these obstacles. Each of these principles has been discussed in other chapters in this book, but here the principles are examined through the lens of sustainability. The third and final part offers guidance on how to apply those principles in each of the five phases of the advising mission.

The Lack of Time: A Major Obstacle to Sustainability

Numerous factors can undercut efforts to develop a sustainable improvement in capacity. Most of these have already been discussed in earlier chapters: a lack of cultural sensitivity; a lack of respect for local ownership; an inability or unwillingness to play a supportive, rather than a leading, role; a preference for Western or cookie-cutter solutions; a failure to nurture relationships with local officials and other local actors; conflicting mandates; and so forth. Together, these deficiencies can be summed up as a lack of adequate capacity-building skills.

One impediment to sustainability, however, has largely escaped mention in earlier chapters and merits some discussion here: a lack of time. Even an adviser equipped with otherwise adequate capacity-building skills will find it challenging to contribute to a sustainable solution unless he has enough time to make a lasting difference.

Short tours in a country compounded by leave and security considerations limit access to counterparts and to the environment overall. Less time with the counterpart and other relevant actors means that the adviser has limited opportunities to assess, learn, and signal that he wishes to be a resource, to establish a peer-to-peer relationship, and to identify ideas to strengthen capacity. The result is often either a complete lack of accomplishment or a record of merely superficial accomplishment.[1] And superficial solutions are seldom sustainable. This problem is well known, both to the development community and to the recipients of foreign assistance. The latter have complained for many years that aid agencies should "invest the necessary time," "go more slowly," and "listen to people" in order to "learn about the real circumstances," "get to know people," and "show respect for people's ideas and opinions."[2]

The cost of insufficient time to build capacity is the implementation of unsustainable new systems. The obvious solution is a revised approach to foreign assistance that

- puts a premium on establishing a productive relationship with the relevant actors on the ground;
- makes it a priority to learn, assess, and understand the dynamics on the ground;
- recognizes that identifying and sharing relevant expertise takes time, as does the preparation of plans for implementing changes; and
- builds into schedules the time needed to troubleshoot the unintended consequences of the implementation of plans.

The authority to make these kinds of changes seldom resides with an adviser. Hence, the effective adviser is usually obliged to operate within tight—overly tight—deadlines. The effective adviser understands this reality, however, and works to mitigate the negative effects of shorter than desired tours. How, exactly, does he achieve this? By respecting the principles laid out in the following section.

Six Principles for Fostering Sustainability

Many of the principles that have been presented throughout the book as the keys to effective advising are also the keys to creating sustainable solutions. This fact testifies to the holistic nature of an adviser's mission: every facet of the adviser's work should resonate with and build on other facets; each phase of the adviser's mission should build on the preceding phases and set the stage for the following phases.

Incorporate Sustainability into Mandates and Strategies

Sustainability is not an afterthought or an add-on; if sustainability is to be achieved, its importance must be recognized even before the adviser is deployed and its substance nurtured at every phase of that deployment.

Advisers will be most effective when the strategies and plans that outline and define their mission and goals include provisions and caveats that promote sustainable decisionmaking. If the strategists and planners do not explicitly mention sustainability, they should at the very least not demand quick results—the sort of results that can be achieved only by the adviser insisting that local actors adopt cookie-cutter, and therefore unsustainable, solutions.

As this book has emphasized, the adviser needs to spend time listening, observing, and learning in the first phases of his relationship with the counterpart. This activity will help the adviser discover existing capacity and gaps in capacity that will in turn inspire the projects that the adviser will work on with the counterpart. The more that the adviser learns and understands about a situation, the more likely it is that she will be able to formulate advice that fits the local context and thus contributes to the development of a sustainable solution. Unfortunately, donor agencies that deploy advisers tend to be impatient and to regard this learning phase as unproductive. Advisers often complain that they have too little time to develop professional relationships and an in-depth understanding of the local environment because they are required to accomplish and report concrete progress, such as numbers of people trained or types of equipment donated.

Capacity-building strategies should be adjusted in one or both of two ways: to define and measure progress more broadly, and to shift the overall strategy of capacity building so that instead of importing "solutions" from other systems, it tasks the adviser with solving problems by institutionalizing change. Strategies and plans should reflect the need to gain an in-depth understanding of a given situation. For instance, advisers should be asked to report on intangible but vital progress such as identifying a point of entry to discuss a gap in capacity with a counterpart, gaining the support of the counterpart as a cultural adviser, or acquiring a reputation with counterparts as a valuable resource.

In addition, strategists and planners should focus a mission's capacity-building energies not on the operational level but on the institutional level. In most governments that receive aid from the international community, senior officials—those with the power to make institutional reforms—are reticent to change. Rather than confront this reluctance to reform, the donor community often accedes to it and devises missions that target the operational level, where senior officials are seldom found. For example, in security-sector reform assistance missions, most of the donor contributions involve sending weapons, ammunition, and protective gear for police or soldiers and providing them with operational training. This approach is not sustainable because equipment breaks and gets misplaced and trainees move on. A sustainable approach to reform involves senior officials introducing institutional reforms such as the creation of a mechanism to administer and manage operations.[3]

Activities that engage individuals at the operational level are static interventions that strengthen the capacity only of the individuals present. For example, a training workshop on human rights offered to a police force by a foreign agency may educate those police officers who participate in the workshop, and those officers may apply what they have learned in their working lives by showing greater respect for the human rights of suspects. But if those officers are later promoted or leave the police force, their posts will be filled by new recruits who have not been trained in human rights.

This problem is common and suggests that programs offered by international donors should be retooled so that they institutionalize new norms, values, and practices. For example, instead of offering short-lived training programs on human rights to police officers, donors should seek to integrate respect for human rights into the procedures and policies of the police force and strengthen the capacity of the ministry of interior to implement them throughout that force. The advising mission should be reformulated so as to give government institutions guidance on how to modify their practices to make them independent of the individuals supporting operations at the time of the foreign assistance.

Strive to Create Resilient, Flexible Systems

Resilience is essential in capacity-building missions because capable institutions are resilient. The effective adviser helps develop the capacity of government to respond to shocks to the system, so that in the event of a new crisis the country will flex rather than snap. Resilience is essentially a conflict management capacity; more resilience means more capacity to respond to crises in ways that dissuade violence. As a USAID report issued in 2012 explains, resilience is "the ability of people, households, communities, countries, and systems to mitigate, adapt to, and recover from shocks in a manner that reduces chronic vulnerability and facilitates inclusive growth."[4] The goal of the ministerial adviser is to help systems become resilient.

Seek Home-Grown Definitions of Problems and Home-Grown Solutions

A solution is not sustainable if the counterpart and his staff do not embrace it. A so-called solution imposed on a resistant staff is likely to be implemented poorly and may even be sabotaged. The staff, as well as the counterpart, must thus buy into the solution, which means that they must participate in the identification of both problems and solutions. The solutions that will last the longest are those that are homegrown. The declaration that change is necessary and the ideas for how best to effect change must come from local actors, especially those with the power to make change happen. The adviser's role is to facilitate discussion and brainstorming among staff, to help identify a way forward but not to dictate the path to be taken—to convince but not to coerce the counterpart.

Getting buy-in requires that the adviser facilitate (using the facilitation skills discussed in Chapter 4) the development of a plan to fill a gap and that the counterpart and his staff implement and maintain the gap-filling measure. Once a counterpart and staff have agreed that change is necessary, why it is necessary, what needs to be changed, and, in broad terms, how it should be changed, then the adviser can help refine the plan by offering ideas based on her own experience and expertise. But here again, the counterpart and staff must be able to accept or reject the adviser's suggestions and to make the final decision as to how to fill a gap, which resources to exploit, what procedures to amend, and what process to use. For example, an adviser might suggest to a counterpart that the ministry acquire a computer on which to create a database for inventory of material. The counterpart, however, knows that the levels of literacy and numeracy among his staff are low and suspects that many staff members will not use the computer. The adviser therefore suggests that inventory reports feature pictures of computer equipment alongside boxes in which staff can put the number of each type of equipment, rather than using technical descriptions of the equipment and complicated spreadsheets.

Ensure Solutions Are Applicable and Viable

Long-term change is embedded in the realm of the possible. New practices or procedures have to be applicable to the problem as identified by local actors and viable in terms of using resources that are available locally and will continue to be available locally over the long term. An applicable solution is one that will have a concrete impact on existing practices and their outcomes. A solution that is not applicable often becomes a parallel system that is supported by the international intervention and that disappears soon after international actors leave the country. An example of parallel systems is formal and informal systems of justice operating simultaneously and serving different sectors of the population. The international community may believe that formal systems are the solution for enhancing access to justice, but local actors may prefer to continue using the informal system solution, because it is adequate for the context and more familiar. The effective adviser seeks to identify the most applicable solution given the resources, attitudes, norms, and existing practices of key stakeholders.

To be sustainable, a new system or practice must tap existing political, social, capital, and human resources. Human resources are extremely important to maintaining the proper functioning of a system. Besides needing the buy-in of the staff of an institution or the operators of a service (e.g., doctors, educators, police, soldiers, border agents, judges), sustainability depends on the ability of current staff members to contribute effectively to the new normal and on the ability of the general population to access the new services. There is no point introducing a computerized solution to a problem if the computer skills of the staff are limited and unlikely to be enhanced for the foreseeable future, and if the general population is largely illiterate. The future availability of human resources—in terms not only of numbers of personnel but also of their education and skills—must also be considered.

Human and capital resources are typically scarce in transitioning societies, but some donor agencies and some advisers seem to forget this fact when designing programs or seem to harbor the illusion that resources will become far more abundant in the future. It is better to scale back the scope of a program than to make it reliant on human and capital resources that are not present. A solution that relies on conditions other than the ones currently existing in the environment is highly likely to cease to function when the additional resources furnished by the international donor community dry up.

Capital resources are as important as human resources. Capital resources include domestic and international funds to cover the operational costs of new programs implemented by any change in a system. However, no program is sustainable if it cannot be supported financially from the coffers of the government. The effective adviser ensures that the operational costs of running a program or system are not dependent on international funds. International funds may be used in many cases to fund the setting up of a new system, but the budget for its operation must be found locally.

Nurture Inclusivity

The effective adviser engages as many local actors as her position permits and encourages and supports the development of systematic interaction between different groups of local stakeholders, especially between government service provider groups and those who would benefit from a government service (e.g., police and the public).[5]

The effective adviser also encourages her counterpart and other leaders within the institution to develop a bold message with compelling reasons for doing things differently. Setting the stage for acceptance of change involves establishing a sense of urgency. Leaders often underestimate how hard it can be to drive people out of their comfort zones. Indeed, they can soon forget how difficult it was for themselves to become convinced of the need for reform. Sometimes getting a change off the ground is the hardest part of the process.

Once a sense of urgency has been created, along with a mind-set that the status quo is untenable and more unappealing than change, the adviser can shepherd the leader and staff through the next phases of change management: forming a coalition of institutional insiders who support the change and can help shape it, creating a shared vision, communicating it, empowering others, creating short-term wins, consolidating improvements, and finally institutionalizing new approaches.[6] Throughout this process, the adviser must seek to promote inclusivity and nurture the belief that the change will benefit everyone. For instance, the adviser might recommend bringing together staff members who do not normally interact and asking them for their ideas. Such meetings often lead to the brainstorming of ideas that would never have been voiced without face-to-face interaction.[7] Additionally, these informal interactions give an opportunity to quickly rebut false assumptions about the change, such as the belief that change will benefit only senior staff. Studies have shown that assumptions that are not promptly countered will be regarded as fact, leading people to ignore data that do not tally with their false belief.[8]

Cope with Resistance to Change

The advising mission will almost always face considerable resistance to the change it is trying to help bring about. Resistance may come from the leadership of the institution, from staff and those who deliver a government service (e.g., police, teachers, doctors), and from the users of the service, whether it is the entire population, as is the case with the police and the military, or a targeted population such as children receiving education. In some cases, resistance is difficult to identify; counterparts may go along with reforms, but if they are not an integral part of both the decisionmaking and the implementation processes, they will not strengthen their capacity to adapt and develop an ability to cope with the inevitable barrage of obstacles to change.

Resistance tends to be inspired by three factors: poor or nonexistent coordination of reform efforts; fear of the complexity of change; and a discomfort with the uncertainty that transition brings about.

Advising missions can overlap and have unintended consequences on one another if coordination is not undertaken by the various advisers working on related but independent projects. For example, a project to usher in a new policy for a police force (e.g., to determine what type of response to use in specific situations) will influence the training that takes place. Coordination between policy change and training change is necessary if both changes are to lead to sustainable good practices. It is important to remember that policy changes set in motion a process of change that ends with a new way of operating. The effective adviser is mindful that related reform efforts must not only be coherent in themselves but must also cohere with one another. A lack of coherence and consistency can confuse counterparts about the validity and the value of the changes being made and encourage suspicions that outsiders are ruining an indigenous institution, which invariably leads to opposition to a changed practice or procedure.

The complexity of the process and dynamics of change can quickly become overwhelming to the targets of change, those whose behavior, practices, and activities are the focus of reform. Complexity can also fuel a suspicion (one that is accurate in many cases) that reforms are making matters worse rather than better. The effective adviser thus invests considerable time in establishing forums in which to regularly discuss progress and unintended consequences that need to be mitigated. A lack of communication with stakeholders and a failure to take the pulse of the process of change sends the message that change is haphazard and unmanaged. The effective adviser also shares information with the counterpart every step of the way, reporting regularly on advances and setbacks so that the counterpart continues to feel that the adviser is a useful resource but is not trying to take control of the change process. Keeping the counterpart in the dark or at bay signals a lack of respect both for his status and for the counterpart's contributions to the process of reform.

Change can exact very high costs, or at least can seem to do so to officials, staff, and other stakeholders with a vested interest in the existing system. Change ushers in a transitional phase that is characterized by uncertainty and ridden with unexpected challenges. These challenges can make the recipients and targets of change doubt if the decision to allow change was a good one. This lack of conviction will gradually weaken their commitment to making the change stick. For example, a deputy minister who agrees to streamline a procurement policy may regret doing so when the problems that the old policy was controlling begin to manifest themselves. Effective advisers prepare counterparts and others to anticipate negative consequences of change and to respond to them by devising new methods to address both old and new problems. Effective advisers remain directly involved throughout the implementation phase of the project to assist in dealing with negative consequences.

Promoting Sustainability in All Five Phases of the Adviser's Mission

This section offers guidance on how to apply these principles at each of the five stages of the adviser-counterpart relationship. Sustainability is or should be a concern throughout the adviser's mission; if the adviser does not incorporate sustainability into phase 1, the mission will never progress to phase 2, and if sustainability is neglected in phase 2, the mission will not reach phase 3—and so on. Recognizing this fact is the starting point for creating enduring solutions.

The effective adviser plans for her tour according to the five-phase framework, anticipating spending about one-fifth of her time on each phase but also recognizing that the phases will overlap, in some cases considerably. For instance, while assessing the local environment and establishing a productive relationship with the counterpart are the major activities in phase 1, they will continue throughout the adviser's tour. The adviser should ensure that she devotes enough attention to identify and understand the relevant dynamics and opportunities present at *each* phase. For example, devoting considerable time to the planning of a project with a counterpart (phase 4) does not guarantee that the implementation of that plan (phase 5) will go smoothly; phase 5 will also require the adviser to be actively involved to troubleshoot problems and help the new system or procedure take root.

Many returning advisers report having spent too much time overcoming obstacles, such as getting access to busy counterparts and eroding officials' resistance to change, and not enough time seeking to understand the problems, issues, and gaps to be addressed.[9] Time management is made even more challenging by the relative brevity of an adviser's deployment. For this reason, the effective adviser practices the skills that she will need in a country before being deployed. Becoming fully attuned before deployment to the many principles and tools of effective advising will enable an adviser to hit the ground running.[10]

Phase 1: Initial Meetings with the Counterpart

The effective adviser builds in the principle of sustainability from the onset of her tour. The adviser needs to be highly aware of sustainability as a concept and to shape all of her activities and contributions with sustainability in mind. Before starting an advising tour, therefore, the effective adviser makes a list of the components of a sustainable system and uses this list as a measuring stick to evaluate the activities to which she will contribute. The adviser, however, should not be tied down to a *specific* system. The precise nature of the system should be determined by local needs, interests, resources, constraints, and so forth. The adviser might ask herself: What are the key components of a system that would efficiently maintain police equipment? The answer lies in the idea that a system provides a service to those who need it to perform their duties effectively. If the police have equipment that can be checked out during their time on duty and returned for maintenance and recharging, what type of system can enable that? What types of threats are there to the attainment of this vision? How can a system guard against those?

Phase 2: Identification and Definition of the Problem

Sustainability is built in when the problem is identified by the counterpart, explained by the counterpart, and demonstrated by the counterpart. Letting the counterpart take the lead teaches the adviser the angle from which the counterpart approaches the problem, what is important to the counterpart, what specific obstacles the counterpart expects to encounter in addressing the problem, and where the counterpart believes potential resistance may lie. This listening and observing period allows the adviser to learn a great deal about the situation, the risks of action and inaction, and the point of entry or angle from which to introduce ideas for addressing the issues.

This phase requires time and patience, but it is one of the most rewarding investments an adviser can make. Countless advisers have reported having to conclude this problem-identification phase too soon, because reporting requirements forced them to advance swiftly to the solution-identification phase. Ideally, a mission's strategists and planners will modify reporting requirements to permit a lengthier phase 2.

Phase 3: Identification of a Solution

Once a solution has been selected as a result of an exploratory period of sharing ideas by the adviser and vetting of those ideas by the counterpart for their viability, the adviser will have to seek buy-in from the counterpart, staffs, and any other decision-makers who must approve the solution. Getting buy-in is possible only if the adviser has diligently sought to facilitate the identification and definition of the problem by the counterpart. The most sustainable solution is the one that is able to recognize the dynamics that may obstruct the desired change and to mitigate their impact.

It is also important to secure buy-in from those who will be the end users of the new service. If, for example, a bus service is being established to transport children to a clinic where they can be vaccinated, the children's parents should be consulted to discover their opinions of where, when, and how the new service should operate. If the end user fails to use the service because it is not accessible or because it challenges beliefs, values, and goals of the public, the change will be inherently unsustainable—as well as a foolish investment.

Phase 4: Development of a Plan to Address the Situation

When, and only when, a particular solution has been accepted and welcomed by the relevant officials, staff members, and other stakeholders, a capacity-building plan should be drafted. Sustainability is built into the plan when it considers (1) funding human capital, (2) the structure of the institution, (3) the culture and the historical context, and (4) the circumstances that have prompted foreign assistance.

Planning must consider the existing level of capacity of individuals and institutions and seek to build on that level; planners must not pretend that a staff or the wider population can suddenly leap from a very low level to a very high level. For example, if a new system requires a literate, computer literate, and numerate population, that system will not be sustainable in a country where nine out of ten people are illiterate. It is possible to train people to make a system work, but if the next generation of staff will not have the same skills, the system will no longer be maintained and the services it provides will falter. The consequence of such a failure will be an erosion of trust in the government—and in a transitional society, the legitimacy of a government is too fragile to risk eroding.

Phase 5: Implementation of the Plan

The implementation stage is just as crucial for sustainability as the other phases—and just as likely to feature obstacles and setbacks. In addition to a simple but often widespread reluctance to change, typical obstacles include:

- Personnel changes, especially those that are not merit based and that bring in individuals who have little understanding of the needs.
- Political maneuvering after buy-in has been established.
- Realization by the counterpart, staff, and/or end users of the costs of change.
- Reluctance to accept expertise from outsiders and skepticism that such expertise is relevant to local circumstances.

While a good plan mitigates for unforeseen consequences and attempts to minimize them, unexpected problems will surely arise. Faced with unanticipated problems, many advisers have reported that they have resorted to cookie-cutter stopgap measures to save the project, tainting the carefully customized plan that had been accepted by local actors and deemed viable for the local context. The resulting patchwork solution is likely to contain parts that are no longer dependent solely on local resources. And while some degree of buy-in may have been achieved, the pain of change will inevitably make some less willing to continue to support the plan or collaborate in its implementation. The approaches that are used to troubleshoot problems during implementation have to be sustainable. The effective adviser understands the value of taking the time to identify local solutions that can rely in both the short and the long term on local resources to address an obstacle encountered during implementation.

Notes

1. Anthony H. Cordesman, *Failing Transition: The New 2013 Report on Progress Toward Security and Stability in Afghanistan* (Washington, DC: Center for Strategic and International Studies, August 5, 2013).

2. CDA Collaborative Learning Projects, "Lessons Learned from Past Experience for International Agencies in Haiti" (Cambridge, MA: CDA Collaborative Learning Projects, n.d.), http://reliefweb.int/report/haiti/lessons-learned-past-experience-international-agencies-haiti (accessed October 30, 2013).

3. David Bayley and Robert Perito, *Police in War: Fighting Insurgency, Terrorism, and Violent Crime* (Boulder, CO: Lynne Rienner, 2010), 154–158.

4. USAID, *Building Resilience to Recurrent Crisis: USAID Policy and Program Guidance* (Washington, DC: USAID, December 2012), http://www.usaid.gov/sites/default/files/documents/1870/USAIDResiliencePolicyGuidanceDocument.pdf (accessed October 31, 2013).

5. A. Heather Coyne, *Empowering Local Peacebuilders: Strategies for Effective Engagement of Local Actors in Peace Operations,* Building Peace no. 2. (Washington, DC: United States Institute of Peace, 2012).

6. Ibid.

7. Michael Beer and Nitin Nohria, "Cracking the Code of Change," *Harvard Business Review* (May-June 2000).

8. Robert Kegan and Lisa Lashkow Lahey, "The Real Reason People Won't Change," *Harvard Business Review* (November 2011): 51–64.

9. Author's interviews with returning advisers, conducted in 2012 and 2013, Washington, DC.

10. Comments by General David Petraeus, Cdr NTM_A Afghanistan, in response to request for feedback by MoDA instruction team, 2011.

11

Exiting

THIS FINAL CHAPTER LOOKS AT THE END OF THE ADVISER'S deployment, and more particularly at what the adviser can do to enhance continuity of the project or projects on which she has been working. Capacity building is a long-term endeavor (conventional wisdom states that real change takes a generation to take hold), and in many cases the advising mission continues well beyond the tour of one adviser. The transition from one adviser to another carries with it a high risk of the exiting adviser's capacity-building projects slowing down or even coming to a complete halt.

To avoid such a break, an adviser must build continuity into her activities. "Continuity" in this context means seeing one's work as part of a longer-term mission and putting in place mechanisms that will enable incoming advisers to swiftly and smoothly assume responsibility for ongoing projects. Most missions, however, do not require advisers to plan for continuity, and thus it is up to the adviser to shoulder this task. Fortunately, advisers want their work to count, to have made a difference, and thus are usually willing to accept this responsibility. What they need, though, is guidance in how best to foster continuity.

To that goal, continuity planning is crucial. Continuity planning is done by documenting the key points of the advising tour.

Continuity Planning and the
Five Phases of an Advising Mission

The key to promoting continuity is continuity planning, which consists of documenting the most important points of an adviser's tour. The five-phases approach to an adviser's mission offers a framework with which to structure the continuity plan. Each phase yields information that can be valuable for incoming advisers,[1] information such as:

- Existing capacity.
- The prior adviser's assessment of opportunities and pitfalls.
- The politics of the local environment.
- National and international constraints.
- The social style and power base of the counterpart.
- Gaps in capacity identified during discussions with the counterpart and staff.
- Which actors have an interest in boycotting or sabotaging change.

Records documenting the first and second phases, which focus on understanding the context and gaps and needs, may not need to be revised just because of a change of guard. An incoming adviser should not rely completely on the outgoing adviser's earlier assessment of the situation, but this assessment should not be completely ignored either. While the development of an effective professional relationship is a process between two individuals, information shared at one time between an outgoing adviser and his counterpart can be helpful for the next adviser seeking to establish a good working partnership with the same counterpart. Of course, exactly what is recorded and how it is recorded will depend in part on the outgoing adviser's social style, experience, expertise, and the contextual factors in play at the time the information was documented.

The information gathered in phase 3, the solution-identification phase, should be comprehensively documented. Information about possible solutions, the counterpart's and staff's own ideas for changes to policies and procedures, and the successes and failures of previous initiatives can make a big difference to the incoming adviser's ability to map the realm of the possible.

During the planning and implementation phases, phases 4 and 5, the outgoing adviser should have recorded any interactions that offered insights into political will, financial constraints, and other salient features of the local landscape. A record of the detours taken and difficulties encountered in the past will not help the incoming adviser avoid all problems in the future, but it should help her to sidestep some pitfalls and decide which options are more promising than others.

Avoiding Redundancy and Repetition

A record of the ideas, considerations, and preoccupations that surfaced in conversations between the outgoing adviser and counterpart will help the incoming adviser avoid asking the same questions as his predecessor. If counterparts and staff recognize that the new adviser has learned nothing from the old adviser, their patience will be tested and their confidence in the new adviser (and in the overall mission) will be eroded. Conversely, an adviser who is able to avoid redundancy and repetition will be more likely to earn the respect of local actors.

An adviser who has facilitated the development of, say, an effective procurement system should record information such as:

- What he has learned about context, constraints, opportunities, resources, reluctance, and resistance.
- What ideas have been tried in the past, an assessment of their impacts (negative and positive), and an evaluation of the reasons for failures and successes of implementation.
- What diagnoses and prescriptions the counterpart, staff, and institution accept and what they reject; what needs they articulate and what problems they want to solve; and how they perceive the impact of a particular problem.
- How resources and culture influence the capacity of local actors and the institution.

Any assessment made by an adviser that goes beyond pure description must outline the adviser's assumptions (e.g., assumptions about the willingness of local actors to buy into a solution) and the reasoning that led the adviser to his conclusions. The content and tone of any adviser's report will reflect his individual understanding of the local environment, mission goals, and so forth. Perceptions of the same environment, of course, can differ widely. For these reasons, continuity documentation is most useful when it focuses on sharing data (e.g., verbatim transcriptions of what was said) rather than opinions and interpretations (e.g., the adviser's assessment of why and how it was said).

Reinforcing the Principles of Advising

Continuity planning helps the adviser who is documenting the five phases to reinforce some of the most important tenets of advising and capacity building. In the first place, the process of regularly documenting information encourages the adviser to test and clarify her interpretation of problems and solutions, because that interpretation has to be presented in a way that will make sense to someone else in the future. Second, the process helps the adviser evaluate her activities in terms of their sustainability. For instance, the adviser is compelled to acknowledge whether she or the counterpart is devising the solution and drafting the plan for implementing it. If the adviser discovers that she is inadvertently undermining the prospects for sustainability, the adviser can redirect her efforts accordingly.

For the incoming adviser, this type of information helps explain why a particular approach was adopted and how the new adviser can build on the progress so far achieved. Continuity of operations and cohesiveness of advising activities builds the confidence of the local officials in the quality of the support they are receiving. By contrast, a lack of such information will disrupt continuity and undermine the progress that has been made, thereby fueling local perceptions that the adviser—and by extension the mission and even the donor community as a whole—is part of the problem, not part of the solution.

Evaluation and Continuity

Continuity planning is also an opportunity to evaluate the activities that are being undertaken.

Continuous evaluation of his own activities by an adviser requires both process evaluation and impact evaluation. *Process eval-*

uation seeks to understand the quality of the project planning and implementation process;[2] it measures the output of the process (e.g., how many vaccines a clinic has administered and how it has administered them). The criteria to assess the adequacy and applicability of the project to the problem include:

- Coherence of the various elements of the proposed solution.
- Ownership and partnership.
- Sustainability.
- Flexibility.
- Location of responsibility.
- Pressure for success and acceptance of possible failure.
- Institutional competence.
- Relationships of trust.

Impact evaluation measures the outcome of the project (e.g., how many children are healthy because they have been vaccinated). Impact is much more difficult to measure than process because it focuses on the extent to which a system is enhanced and gaps in capacity reduced (it is easy to count how many vaccines were administered by a clinic but difficult to measure the impact of those vaccines on people's lives). Measuring impact requires asking the following questions:

- What is the impact in terms of the immediate objectives of the project?
- What is the impact of the project on parties, issues, and other elements of the local environment?
- What is the impact of the transitional environment on the project?
- How has the project changed people's lives? How has the old normal changed for people? What are the improvements in the lives of those who are meant to benefit from the solution that has been implemented?
- How can the project be adjusted or reformulated to make it more effective?

Essentially, impact evaluation requires the adviser to seek to understand how the change that he is helping to implement is contributing to a new normal—to a new system with a new outcome.

*   *   *

Advising is an exploratory process. It involves exploring gaps, solutions, approaches, and relationships. The evaluation of the process that the outgoing adviser has helped to shape should help guide the incoming adviser's explorations as he searches for the best way to build on, rather than undermine or rebuild, what already exists.

Notes

1. A note of caution: Gathering information about the context and dynamics is not the same as gathering intelligence to share with other agencies, domestic or international, that goes beyond the mandate of building capacity. Advisers are not intelligence officers and under no circumstances should engage in such activities, as these are separate from advising and have a high likelihood of being damaging to capacity-building activities.

2. Gordon Crawford with Iain Kearton, "Evaluating Democracy and Governance Assistance," ESCOR Research Report no. 7894 (London: ALNAP, December 2000).

Glossary

Active listening: Active listening (also known as "strategic listening") involves asking specific questions that will lead the discussion toward the goal of attaining specific knowledge or understanding. It means listening for specific information rather than listening to what the interlocutor wishes to share.

Adviser: An adviser is an experienced practitioner who is sent by a foreign country or international organization to help build capacity in institutions in transitional societies. The adviser has no executive function. His role is limited to sharing advice, often in the form of recommendations for reforming or transforming an organization. An adviser typically works alongside a counterpart who is a high-ranking official within a ministry or agency.

Authority: Among the several meanings of authority, two are especially important for an adviser to keep in mind: the power to make decisions and enforce them, and the expertise that a professional possesses and that can be a resource for officials seeking to enhance their performance.

Band-Aid approach: Development assistance that funnels money and expatriates to a country with the goal of foreigners solving local problems by transplanting solutions from other countries and contexts. It does not involve knowledge transfer and, as such, is a superficial remedy. (See also *Cookie-cutter approach.*)

Capacity: The ability of people, institutions, and societies to perform functions, solve problems, and set and achieve objectives. At the organizational level, *capacity* refers to management structures, processes, systems, and practices as well as an institution's relationships with other organizations and sectors, including public, private, and community organizations.

Capacity building: Enabling people, organizations, and societies to develop, strengthen, and expand their abilities to meet their goals or fulfill their mandates. Capacity is strengthened through the transfer of knowledge and skills that enhance individual and collective abilities to deliver services and carry out programs that address challenges in a sustainable way.

Change agent: A change agent understands the dynamics that facilitate or hinder change and, as such, can be a catalyst of change within an organization. In an effective advising mission, the counterpart will alert the adviser as to which staff members have the authority to propose and execute change.

Civil society: A collective term for a wide array of nongovernmental and nonprofit groups that help their society at large function while working to advance their own or others' well-being. Civil society can include civic, educational, trade, labor, charitable, media, religious, recreational, cultural, and advocacy groups, as well as informal associations and social movements.

Co-analysis: An adviser's first task is to get a comprehensive understanding of the capacity in the environment, but she must not do this independently. Co-analysis is the process of identifying and establishing existing capacity with the counterpart.

Conflict: An inevitable aspect of human interaction, conflict is present when two or more individuals or groups pursue mutually incompatible goals. Conflicts can be waged violently, as in a war, or nonviolently, as in an election or an adversarial legal process.

Conflict management: A general term that describes efforts to prevent, limit, contain, or resolve conflicts, especially violent ones, while building up the capacities of all parties involved to undertake peacebuilding.

Conflict sensitivity: Conflict sensitivity means being sensitive to the potential impact of an intervention (e.g., a program) on a specific community. Analysis and assessment can also be forms of intervention that have consequences on an environment.

Cookie-cutter approach: A process by which capacity builders implement, or influence the implementation of, solutions by exporting the systems, processes, and/or procedures that make up their home institutions. (See also *Band-Aid approach*.)

Coordination: Coordination is the act of managing interdependencies between activities that are designed to achieve a particular goal. Failure to coordinate has a negative impact on the larger mission of which an adviser is a part.

Corruption: The abuse of power for private gain, including bribery, extortion, fraud, nepotism, embezzlement, falsification of records, kickbacks, and influence peddling. Although commonly associated with the public sector, it also exists in the business sector and civil society.

Counterpart: The counterpart is the adviser's partner, and the expert on his own systems, processes, and institutions. She is the professional peer of the adviser, and the individual who must initiate and execute any and all reforms. Typically, a counterpart to a strategic advisor is in a leadership position within a government ministry or agency. (An adviser may have several counterparts on a single mission, but this book assumes that the adviser is working with just one counterpart.)

Culture: The shared beliefs, traits, attitudes, behaviors, products, and artifacts common to a particular society or ethnic group. Cultural sensitivity means being aware of cultural differences and how they can affect behavior, and moving beyond cultural biases and preconceptions to interact effectively.

Doer: A doer is a professional who is accustomed to taking action to accomplish practical goals, and who has enjoyed the authority to do so. A doer who becomes an adviser must make the internal transformation from doer to helper.

Do no harm: A maxim that acknowledges that any intervention carries with it the risk of doing harm. In assistance activities, the maxim recognizes that resources inevitably represent the distribution of power and wealth and will create tensions if careful attention is not given to how they are distributed and delivered.

Donor: A donor is a member of the international community that provides development aid. Such assistance is traditionally given to developing countries to support their economic, social, and political development. Such assistance usually comes from individual countries or from international organizations such as the United Nations Development Programme and the World Bank Group.

Effective adviser: The term used in this book to describe an adviser who acts wisely and appropriately and is able to promote sustainable change. (See also *Effective advising mission.*)

Effective advising mission: An effective advising mission is one in which an array of alternative approaches to problem solving and system reform is presented by the adviser to the counterpart with the understanding that the counterpart alone has the authority to accept or reject those approaches. An effective advising mission begins with many information-seeking questions and joint brainstorming sessions and is long enough to enable the adviser and the counterpart to develop a productive rapport.

Empowerment: According to the World Bank, empowerment is the process of enhancing the capacity of individuals or groups to make choices and to transform those choices into desired outcomes.[1] Empowered individuals have the freedom and capacity to participate, negotiate, influence, control, and request accountability from individuals or institutions.

Facilitation: The process or set of skills by which a third party attempts to help disputants move toward resolution of their dispute, including helping the parties set ground rules and meeting agendas. Effective advisers are facilitators who elicit parties to share experiences and to guide the analysis of outcomes of past activities in order to identify and integrate lessons to be applied in the future.

Fragility: Fragile states typically suffer from weak authority, legitimacy, and capacity. Fragile states often have weak economies and struggle with one or more of the following: adhering to the rule of law, controlling territory, respecting minorities, and delivering basic services to the population.

Governance: The exercise of authority to implement rules and policies in an effort to bring order to the social, political, economic, and judicial processes that allow a society to develop. Good governance implies a level of accountability and transparency, both of which will help to ameliorate the risk of corruption, a corrosive and destabilizing practice.

Intervention: An intervention refers to an action by an external actor operating within a host country and intended to effect a change (be it major or minor) within the host country. An intervention can take many forms. It may refer to a full-scale mission—including troops, police, diplomats, aid workers, development specialists, and so forth—dispatched by the international community to a transitional society. It may also refer to any activity undertaken in the host country by an intergovernmental, governmental, or nongovernmental organization, team, or individual that is part of the larger mission.

Knowledge transfer: The process of sharing information and skills with a target audience and enabling them to integrate that knowledge into their daily practice. Three methods of knowledge transfer include prescriptive (transferring technical skills), adaptive (helping counterparts identify a more effective alternative in the absence of one "correct" way of doing things), and elicitive (practicing a skill until it becomes second nature).

Legitimacy: Legitimacy refers to the degree to which the advising activities are part of a widely recognized and formally accepted mandate and are accepted or at least tolerated by the affected population and the host country government. In terms of an adviser's work, legitimacy refers to being perceived by local actors as having the right to be offering assistance; essentially that both countries, donor and recipient, have signaled their intent to engage in some form of foreign assistance project or activities.

Local ownership: The notion that the affected country must drive its own development needs and priorities even if transitional authority is in the hands of outsiders. Local ownership attempts to bridge the asymmetries of the donor-recipient relationship to reach a more equal peacebuilding partnership between outsiders and insiders.

Mentor: Like an adviser, a mentor is a professional from a donor country who works with officials from the host country, but mentorship is not synonymous with advising. Mentors work at the operational, rather than strategic level, offering advice on how to implement policies or how to usher in sustainable change effectively. The term is sometimes seen as condescending, because it implies that the foreigner is coaching the counterpart on how to perform as well as the mentor. (See also *Adviser* and *Trainer.*)

Reform: Refining or improving a process, a system, an institution, or an entire government to ensure it functions effectively.

Rule of law: A principle of governance in which all persons and institutions, public and private, including the state itself, are accountable to laws that are publicly announced, equally enforced and independently adjudicated, and consistent with international human rights norms and standards. In addition, all persons must have the ability to seek and obtain a remedy through informal or formal institutions of justice.

Social capital: Closely related to "human capital," and often used interchangeably, social capital refers to the resources that create a strong network of institutionalized relationships in society. These connections between individuals and between social networks facilitate civic engagement and encourage bargaining, compromise, and pluralistic politics, as well as contribute to economic and social development.

Stability: The ability of a state to recover from disturbances and resist sudden change or deterioration. Stabilization is the process of ending or preventing the recurrence of violent conflict and creating the conditions for normal economic activity and nonviolent politics.

Strategic advising: The deployment of advisers by the international community to build capacity in transitional countries.

Sustainability: In general, the ability to maintain something indefinitely. In capacity building, sustainability means creating capacity that will remain in place and continue to be effective even after the intervention ends or the intervener departs.

System: As defined by scholars of system theory, a system is an organized collection of parts, or subsystems, that are highly integrated to accomplish an overall goal. In this book, systems can range in size and complexity from enormous (e.g., a country's social system) to small (e.g., the system within a ministry for inventorying its computer equipment). International interventions always affect the systems that are in place. An open system absorbs information, which facilitates peer-to-peer advising and knowledge transfer.

Targets of change: Targets of change are individuals without sufficient capacity to perform necessary tasks and achieve desired outcomes. Some targets of change contribute to other people's problems through their actions or lack of actions (e.g., an ineffective police force), and some targets of change experience the problems themselves (e.g., staff members whose work output is not utilized because the bureaucratic system is too disorganized).

Trainer: Trainers help others learn how to effectively implement policies and procedures. They impart knowledge at the operational level and are not involved in brainstorming, strategic visioning, or systems analysis. (See also *Adviser* and *Mentor.*)

Transitional society: A transitional society (or *transitional country*) is a society that is emerging from violent conflict or moving from an authoritarian to a more democratic political system.

Trust: "Trust" is an emotionally fraught term and means different things to different people. The effective adviser will garner professional trust in her expertise and its relevance to the issue that the counterpart is interested in addressing, rather than aim for trust on an interpersonal level.

Source: Most of these definitions are taken from or based on definitions in Daniel Snodderly, ed., *Peace Terms: Glossary of Terms for Conflict Management and Peacebuilding* (Washington, DC: United States Institute of Peace, 2011), http://www.usip.org/sites/default/files/files/peace terms.pdf.

Note: 1. Poverty Reduction Group (PRMPR) of the World Bank's Poverty Reduction and Economic Management Network, *Empowerment in Practice: Analysis and Implementation: A World Bank Learning Module* (Washington, DC: World Bank Institute, 2007).

Bibliography

Abu-Nimer, Mohammed. "Conflict Resolution Training in the Middle East: Lessons to Be Learned." *International Negotiations* 3 (1998): 99–116.

Anderson, Mary B. *Do No Harm: How Aid Can Support Peace—or War.* Boulder, CO: Lynne Rienner, 1999.

Bayley, David, and Robert Perito. *Police in War: Fighting Insurgency, Terrorism, and Violent Crime.* Boulder, CO: Lynne Rienner, 2010.

Beck, Michael. *The 5 Mistakes Executives Most Often Make (And How to Avoid Them).* Executive Briefing. Denver, CO: Exceptional Leadership, Inc., 2005.

Beer, Michael, and Nitin Nohria. "Cracking the Code of Change." *Harvard Business Review* (May-June 2000).

Boege, Volker, Anne Brown, Kevin Clements, and Anna Nolan. "Building Peace and Political Community in Hybrid Political Orders." *International Peacekeeping* 16, no. 5 (2009): 599–615.

Bolton, Robert, and Dorothy G. Bolton. *Social Style–Management Style: Developing Productive Work Relationships.* New York: Amacom, 1984.

Caplan, Richard. "Partner or Patron? International Civil Administration and Local Capacity-Building." *International Peacekeeping* 11, no. 2 (2004).

Chandler, David. *International Statebuilding: The Rise of Post Liberal Governance.* Critical Issues in Global Politics Series. New York: Routledge, 2010.

Cooper, Helen, and Thom Shanker. "U.S. Redefines Afghan Success Before Conference." *New York Times*, May 17, 2012.

Cordesman, Anthony H. *Failing Transition: The New 2013 Report on Progress Toward Security and Stability in Afghanistan.* Washington, DC: Center for Strategic and International Studies, August 5, 2013.

Coyne, A. Heather. *Empowering Local Peacebuilders: Strategies for Effective Engagement of Local Actors in Peace Operations.* Building Peace no. 2. Washington, DC: United States Institute of Peace, 2012.

Crawford, Gordon, with Iain Kearton. "Evaluating Democracy and Governance Assistance." ESCOR Research Report no. 7894 (London: ALNAP, December 2000).

Crocker, Chester. "Peacemaking and Mediation: Dynamics of a Changing Field." Coping with Crisis Working Paper Series. New York: International Peace Academy, 2007.

Department for International Development (DFID). "DFID Research Strategy 2008–2013." Working Paper Series: Capacity Building, 2008.

Dobbins, James. "Who Lost Iraq? Lessons from the Debacle." *Foreign Affairs* 86, no. 5 (September-October 2007): 61–74.

"The European Consensus on Development." *Joint Declaration by the Council and the Representatives of the Governments of the Member States Meeting Within the Council, the European Parliament and the Commission on the Development Policy of the European Union.* April 2006.

Fairclough, Norman. "Critical Discourse Analysis." In *How to Analyse Talk in Institutional Settings*, 25–40. Bodmin: MPG Book Ltd., 2001.

Harris, Peter, and Ben Reilly. *Democracy and Deep-Rooted Conflict: Options for Negotiators.* International IDEA Book Series. Stockholm: IDEA, 1998.

International Security Sector Advisory Team (ISSAT). "Operational Guidance Note: The Security and Justice Sector Reform Adviser." 2013. http://issat.dcaf.ch/content/download/1181/8973/file/ISSAT%20OGN%20%20The%20Security%20and%20Justice%20Reform%20Adviser.pdf (accessed September 2015).

Jennings, Ray S. *The Road Ahead: Lessons in Nation Building from Japan, Germany, and Afghanistan for Postwar Iraq.* Peaceworks no. 49. Washington, DC: United States Institute of Peace, 2009.

Kegan, Robert, and Lisa Lashkow Lahey. "The Real Reason People Won't Change." *Harvard Business Review* (November 2011): 51–64.

Kiraly, Dominic. "Making Meaning Through Interpreters: Lessons Learned in Zones of Conflict." USIP Instruction CD. Washington, DC: United States Institute of Peace, 2011.

Langseth, Peter, Office of Drug Control and Crime Prevention, United Nations Office at Vienna. "Prevention: An Effective Tool to Reduce Corruption." Paper presented at ISPAC Conference "Responding to the Challenge of Corruption." Milan, 1999.

Lederach, John Paul. *Preparing for Peace: Conflict Transformation Across Cultures.* Syracuse, NY: Syracuse University Press, 1995.

Ledwidge, Frank. *Losing Small Wars: British Military Failure in Iraq and Afghanistan.* New Haven, CT: Yale University Press, 2001.

Mac Ginty, Roger. "Against Stabilization." *Stability: An International Journal of Security and Development* 1, no. 1 (2012): 20–30.

McKechnie, Alastair. "Building Capacity in Post-Conflict Countries." *Social Development Notes: Conflict Prevention and Reconstruction No. 14* (World Bank), December 2003.

Metrinko, Michael. "The American Military Advisor." *Middle East Quarterly* 16, no. 2 (Spring 2009): 70–74.

Mizrahi, Yemile. *Capacity Enhancement Indicators: Review of the Literature.* WBI Evaluation Studies. Washington, DC: World Bank Institute, 2004.

Olsen, Karen H. "Why Planned Interventions for Capacity Development in the Environment Often Fail: A Critical Review of Mainstream Approaches." *International Studies of Management and Organization* 36, no. 2 (2006): 104–124.

Olson, G. M., T. W. Malone, and J. B. Smith, eds. *Coordination Theory and Collaboration Technology.* Mahwah, NJ: Erlbaum, 2001.

Organisation for Economic Co-operation and Development. *Improving International Support to Peace Processes: The Missing Piece.* Paris: OECD Publishing, 2012.

Organization Development. *Five Core Theories—Systems Theory—Organisation Development.* Fortitude Development Limited, n.d.

Pam, Jeremiah S. "The Paradox of Complexity: Embracing Its Contribution to Situational Understanding, Resisting Its Temptation in Strategy and Operational Plans." In *Complex Operations: NATO at War and on the Margins of War,* edited by Christopher M. Schnaubelt. NATO Defense College Forum Paper no. 14. Rome: NATO Defense College, Research Division, July 2010.

Perito, Robert. *Special Report:The Interior Ministry's Role in SSR.* Washington, DC: United States Institute of Peace, 2009.

Poverty Reduction Group (PRMPR) of the World Bank's Poverty Reduction and Economic Management Network. *Empowerment in Practice: Analysis and Implementation: A World Bank Learning Module.* Washington, DC: World Bank Institute, 2007.

Ricks, Thomas E. *Fiasco: The American Military Adventure in Iraq.* New York: Penguin Group, 2006.

Rosenblum-Kumar, Gay. *Capacity-Building in Conflict Management.* SPPD Document. United Nations Development Programme (UNDP) Africa Region, 2001.

Saxby, John. *Local Ownership and Development Co-operation: The Role of Northern Civil Society.* Issues Paper. Ottawa: Canadian International Development Assistance, 2003.

Snavely, William, and Ellen Walters. "Differences in Communication Competence in Administrative Social Styles." *Journal of Applied Communication Research* 11, no. 2 (1983).

Snodderly, Daniel, ed. *Peace Terms: Glossary of Terms for Conflict Management and Peacebuilding.* Washington, DC: United States Institute of Peace, 2011.

Solomon, Richard H, and Nigel Quinney. *American Negotiating Behavior:*

Wheeler-Dealers, Legal Eagles, Bullies, and Preachers. Washington, DC: United States Institute of Peace Press, 2010.

Szporluk, Michael. "A Framework for Understanding Accountability of International NGOs and Global Good Governance." *Indiana Journal of Global Legal Studies* 16, no. 339 (2009).

United Nations Development Programme (UNDP). *Capacity Development: A UNDP Primer.* New York: UNDP, 2009.

United Nations General Assembly. "Report on the World Commission on Environment and Development." UN General Assembly Resolution A/RES/42/187, December 11, 1987.

USAID. *Building Resilience to Recurrent Crisis: USAID Policy and Program Guidance.* Washington, DC: US Agency for International Development, December 2012.

USAID. "USAID Local Governance Project Solicitation Number: SOL-176-12-000002." Request for Proposals. Washington, DC: US Agency for International Development, 2012.

US Army. *Multi-Service Tactics, Techniques, and Procedures for Advising Foreign Forces.* FM 3-07/MCRP 3-33.8A/NTTP 3-07.5/AFTTP 3-2.76. n.d.

US Army War College, Peacekeeping and Stability Operations Institute (PKSOI) and the United States Institute of Peace (USIP). *Guiding Principles for Stabilization and Reconstruction.* Washington, DC: USIP, 2009.

Vella, Jane. *Learning to Listen, Learning to Teach: The Power of Dialogue in Educating Adults.* San Francisco: John Wiley & Sons, 2002.

World Bank. *World Development Report 2011: Conflict, Security, and Development.* Washington, DC: World Bank, 2011.

Index

134; lack of coordination among international actors, 120–121; militarization of, 14; skill sets of effective advisers, 24; as targets of change, 72

policy: characteristics of an adviser, 20; impact of capacity building, 14; tiers of capacity building, 9–10

political navigation, realistic expectations of, 42

power dynamics: international versus local bosses, 45–46; nurturing local ownership, 28. *See also* corruption

pragmatism, 53–54

prescriptive method of adult learning, 81–82

principles of an adviser, 27–36

problem solving: advisers' and counterparts' role in identifying a solution, 98; defining the problem, 95–97; developing a plan, 101–103

process evaluation, 31, 148–149

procurement process, 34, 147–148

professionalism: choosing an interpreter, 114–115; developing a professional relationship, 105–106; establishing credibility, 55–56; ingredients of a good relationship, 92; keeping a professional distance, 116; reputation of an adviser, 26

public works, 62–63

rapport, establishing, 107–112

reform, defining, 155

reform sector: local ownership of the reconstruction dynamic, 29–30

regional actors, coordination among, 123

relationship building: advisers facilitating, 77–78; characteristics of an adviser, 20; coordination, 119–120; cultural awareness, 111–112; defense programs, 15;

defining and building trust, 106–107; denationalized models and solutions, 115–116; developing a plan, 101–103, 141–142; developing a professional relationship, 105–106; developing a rapport, 107–111; developing trust with counterparts, 49–50; differing social styles, 108–110; establishing a partnership, 87–88; facilitating conversation, 78–80; five stages of, 92–105; identifying a solution, 98–100, 141; identifying the problem, 95–97, 140–141; implementing the plan, 103–105, 142–143; ingredients of a good relationship, 91–92; initial meetings with the counterpart, 93–95, 140; interpreters, 114–115; keeping a professional distance, 116; language sensitivity, 112–113; relevant questions for assessing local capacity, 64–68; trainers and mentors, 21–23. *See also* coordination; counterparts; resource, adviser as

resistance to change, 137–139

resource, adviser as: developing a plan, 102–103; effective practices, 58; establishing a partnership, 87–88; establishing a rapport, 107–111; identifying the problem, 97; initial meetings with the counterpart, 93–95; transforming a technical expert into an adviser, 25

resource allocation: "do no harm" principle, 32; fostering local ownership, 30–31; realistic expectations, 42

respect: developing a professional relationship, 105–106; establishing legitimacy of the adviser, 57; guiding principles of an adviser, 28; identifying a solution, 99; implementing the plan, 103–104; for local capacity,

About the Book

THOUGH ADVISERS TO HOST GOVERNMENTS HAVE BECOME AN integral part of foreign-assistance efforts in the realms of both development and peace processes, there has been scant information on how they can best achieve their goals. What skills, tools, and attributes do successful advisers need? How can they best share their expertise with their foreign counterparts in ways that build local capacities and contribute to sustainable solutions?

Filling the lacunae, Nadia Gerspacher's welcome handbook offers practical, step-by-step guidance for any adviser joining an assistance mission tasked with effective and long-lasting local capacity building.

Nadia Gerspacher is director of security sector education at the United States Institute of Peace, where she manages a wide range of capacity-building projects as well as programs that prepare advisers to deploy on capacity-building missions.

171